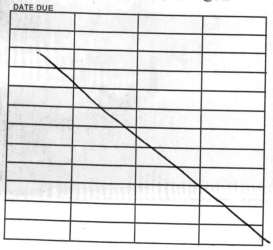

TWAYNE'S WORLD AUTHORS SERIES

A Survey of the World's Literature

Sylvia E. Bowman, Indiana University

GENERAL EDITOR

FRANCE

Maxwell A. Smith, Guerry Professor of French, Emeritus
The University of Chattanooga
Former Visiting Professor in Modern Languages
The Florida State University

EDITOR

Louis Aragon

(TWAS 114)

TWAYNE'S WORLD AUTHORS SERIES (TWAS)

*The purpose of TWAS is to survey the major writers
–novelists, dramatists, historians, poets, philosophers, and
critics–of the nations of the world. Among the national
literatures covered are those of Australia, Canada, China,
Eastern Europe, France, Germany, Greece, Italy, Japan,
Latin America, New Zealand, Poland, Russia, Scandinavia,
Spain, and the African nations, as well as Hebrew, Yiddish,
and Latin Classical literature. This survey is complemented
by Twayne's United States Authors Series and
English Authors Series.*

*The intent of each volume in these series is to present a
critical-analytical study of the works of the writer; to include
biographical and historical material that may be necessary for
understanding, appreciation, and critical appraisal of the
writer; and to present all material in clear, concise
English–but not to vitiate the scholarly content of the work
by doing so.*

Louis Aragon

By LUCILLE F. BECKER
Drew University

Twayne Publishers, Inc.   ::   New York

Preface

Louis Aragon has been described by a prominent French literary critic as "one of the most gifted writers, one of the most dazzling comets to have ever crossed our literary sky."[1] This reputation has been built on a vast literary production. Aragon has published over sixty complete books, including novels, poetry, history, works on esthetics, as well as art and literary criticism, prefaces, newspaper articles, and translations from English and Russian.

While he is well known to his fellow countrymen, his literary reputation in English-speaking countries is limited and is based largely upon a few of his novels. The reasons for this neglect have been several; principal among them are the scarcity of translations of his work and the unpopularity of his political ideology. Only five of his novels and an anthology of his war poetry have been published in English. Even in France, very little critical material has appeared on Aragon other than in the Communist press, which hailed all of his work indiscriminately. It was only with the publication of *La Semaine sainte* in 1958 that the non-Communist critics rediscovered this master of the French language. It has been said of Aragon that "no one embodies with more brilliance, virtuosity, and grace this perfect possession of the resources offered by the language which is, perhaps after all, the essence of literature."[2]

It would be impossible to deal with all of Aragon's literary production within the scope offered by the present study. I shall, instead, provide an introduction to Aragon's major works, dealing with them as nearly as possible in the order in which they appeared in an effort to show their evolution. It will be seen that all of his works, from his early Surrealist poetry to his later works governed by the doctrine of Socialist Realism, are characterized by their preoccupation with the harmonies existing between men's souls and great historical movements as well as by their search for an absolute. "I have always believed that it was my duty to reach the summit/As if I carried all of humanity with me."[3]

In this study, I have drawn heavily from Aragon's works in an effort to present him as much as possible in his own words, to permit him to demonstrate what he calls the "precious power of the poet to express what has as yet been unformulated, and what is impossible to formulate, to set down and describe the terrible, fugitive human experience."[4]

LUCILLE F. BECKER

Drew University

Acknowledgments

I am particularly grateful to Editions Gallimard for its kind and generous permission to quote from the works of Louis Aragon.

Contents

Chronology

1897   Louis Aragon born in Paris, October 3.

1909   July 23. Aragon receives as a prize the volume *Vingt-cinq années de littérature française*, in which he discovers the work of Maurice Barrès.

1914–   Passes baccalauréat examinations in Latin and sciences; then in
1916   philosophy.

1916   Enrolls in preparatory year for medical studies. Begins to write verses which are published during the war in magazines like *Sic* and *Les Fruits nouveaux*. Frequents avant-garde bookshop of Adrienne Monnier on rue de l'Odéon.

1917   Mobilized. Meets André Breton at Val-de-Grâce.

1918   Leaves for the front as "auxiliary doctor" in the infantry. August 13, awarded Croix de guerre.

1919   Occupation of Saar and Rhineland with his regiment. Founds magazine *Littérature* with André Breton and Philippe Soupault in March, under auspices of Paul Valéry, published by Adrienne Monnier.

1920   Publishes his first collection of poems, *Feu de joie*. On November 15, the day after the Socialist Congress at Tours, Aragon thinks about joining Communist party but abandons the idea at that time.

1921   Publication of *Anicet ou le Panorama roman*.

1922   Publication of *Les Aventures de Télémaque*.

1923   Travels in Germany inspired *Les Plaisirs de la Capitale*, published in Berlin.
        Publication of first issue of *La Révolution surréaliste*.

1924   *Le Libertinage* published.
        Une Vague de Rêves published in *Commerce*, Autumn 1924.

1926   "Le Cahier noir" fragment of unpublished novel *La Défense de l'Infini* in *La Revue européenne*, February.
        Publication of *Le Paysan de Paris* and *Le Mouvement perpétuel*.

1927   January 6, joins Communist party.

1928   Translation with preface of *The Hunting of the Snark* by Lewis Carroll. Publication of *Le Traité du style*. Participates in Paris manifestations protesting execution of Sacco and Vanzetti. November 4, meets Mayakovsky at the Coupole. November 5, meets Elsa Triolet at the same café.

1929   Publication of *La Grande Gaieté.*

1930   *La Peinture au défi.* Attends Second International Congress of Revolutionary Writers in Kharkov. Writes poem, "Front Rouge," for *Littérature de la Révolution Mondiale*, publication of the International Writers' Union.

1930–   Several trips to the Soviet Union.
1936

1931   Publication of first issue of *Le Surréalisme au service de la Révolution. Persécuté persécuteur* published. Aragon breaks with Surrealists.

1933–   Newspaperman for Communist newspaper *L'Humanité.*
1934

1934   Publication of *Les Cloches de Bâle* and *Hourra l'Oural.*

1935   Foundation of International Association of Writers for the Defense of Culture. Secretaries of the French section were Jean-Richard Bloch, André Chamson, André Malraux, and Louis Aragon.

1935   *Pour un réalisme socialiste* published.

1936   Aragon and Elsa travel to Russia to see Gorky. They are unable to see him, but attend his funeral. On boat to Russia, Aragon finishes *Les Beaux Quartiers. Les Beaux Quartiers* awarded Prix Renaudot.

1937   Aragon and Elsa leave for Spain to give to Spanish intellectuals gifts from the French section of the International Association of Writers for the Defense of Culture. Communist newspaper, *Ce Soir*, founded. Co-directors Aragon and Jean-Richard Bloch.

1939   Aragon writes editorial in *Ce Soir* defending Russo-German Pact. Paper outlawed by French government. Aragon takes refuge in the Chilean Embassy in Paris, where he writes last one hundred and fifty pages of *Les Voyageurs de l' impériale* and sends it to an American publisher. September 2, Aragon is mobilized in a "Workers Regiment" in which are placed all those who are politically suspect. Aragon invents a key to open tanks from the outside to permit the evacuation of wounded when tanks are hit. For this he receives a letter of commendation from the War Ministry.

1940	Evacuated at Dunkirk on June 1. Returns to France with third light motorized division. Receives Croix de guerre and Médaille Militaire.
1941	With Elsa in Nice. Together with her and Jean Paulhan, Aragon founds the National Committee of Writers. Publication of *Le Crève-coeur. Cantique à Elsa.*
1942	Publication of *Les Voyageurs de l' impériale, Les Yeux d'Elsa,* and *Brocéliande.*
1943	Foundation in Lyons of movement "Les Etoiles," clandestine movement of intellectuals based on cells of five people. Travels to coordinate activities of the National Committee of Writers. July, Aragon and Elsa leave Lyons which has become dangerous for them and go to Drôme region where they found clandestine newspaper, *La Drôme en armes.* Publication of *Le Musée Grévin, En Français dans le texte.*
1944	Publication of *Aurélien.*
1945	Publication of *La Diane française, En Etrange pays dans mon pays lui-même, Servitude et grandeur des Français.*
1946	*L'Enseigne de Gersaint, L'Homme Communiste* (Vol. I), *Apologie du luxe* published.
1947	Publication of *Chroniques du Bel Canto.* Translation of *Five Sonnets by Petrarch,* with a preface.
1947– 1949	Editor of *Ce Soir.*
1948	*Le Nouveau Crève-coeur.* Aragon deprived of civil rights for ten years. Participates in "Battle of the Books," an attempt to disseminate books to the workers and set up book stores throughout France.
1949	On staff of *Les Lettres Françaises.* Publication of *Les Communistes* (Vols. I, II).
1950	Elected temporary member of the Central Committee of the French Communist Party. *Les Communistes* (Vol. III). Aragon sets up program with Gallimard for the translation into French and publication of a collection of contemporary Russian works.
1951	*Les Communistes* (Vol. IV, Vol. V in two parts).
1952	Publication of *Avez-vous lu Victor Hugo? Hugo, poète réaliste, L'Exemple de Courbet.*
1953	Director of *Les Lettres Françaises* after demise of *Ce Soir. L'Homme Communiste* (Vol. II). *Le Neveu de M. Duval. La Lumière de Stendhal.*
1954	Becomes permanent member of the Central Committee of the

nationale, Mes Caravanes et autres poèmes, Les Yeux et la mémoire.

1955   Publication of *Littératures soviétiques.*

1956   *Introduction aux littératures soviétiques* and *Le Roman inachevé.*

1957   Awarded Lenin Peace Prize.

1958   Publication of *La Semaine sainte.*

1959   Publication of *Elsa, J'Abats mon jeu, Entretiens sur le musée de Dresde* (with Jean Cocteau). Translation of *Djamilia* by Aitmatov, with preface.

1960   *Les Poètes.*

1961   Essay on Elsa's work "Elsa Triolet présentée par Aragon."

1962   *Histoire parallèle (U.R.S.S.–U.S.A.)* with André Maurois (four volumes).

1963   *Le Fou d'Elsa* published. Receives honorary doctorate from the University of Prague.

1963–   Ten radio interviews with Francis Crémieux which were pub-
1964   lished by Gallimard in 1964 under the title *Entretiens avec Francis Crémieux.*

1964   *Le Voyage de Hollande.*

1965   Honorary doctorate, University of Moscow. *La Mise à mort* and *Les Collages* published.

1966   *Elégie à Pablo Neruda.* February 16, writes article in *L'Humanité* attacking Soviet Union for its sentencing of writers Andrei Sinyavsky and Daniel.

1967   *Blanche ou l'oubli* published.

1968   Aragon joins with French Communist Party in condemning Russian aggression against Czechoslovakia.

1970   Death of Elsa Triolet on June 16.

CHAPTER 1

"Words Took Me by the Hand"

I Early Influences

"I dream about the way in which a life unfolds, how it seems to develop on its own, without any connection with public affairs or the history of the world. Then it becomes a part of history, from which it borrows its essential characteristics, its direction, its flow."[1] Rarely have the life and work of a writer been as inextricably linked as they have been for Louis Aragon, whose work reflects the principal trends of thought of the twentieth century. As the century has evolved, so has his work which has been a mirror of his time, reflecting the growth of a writer of genius from the nihilistic responses of the youthful Dadaists to his acceptance of the role of a responsible, social citizen. There may be traced in Aragon's novels, essays, and poems the transition from the narrowly individualistic to the vitally collective. Throughout his life, his writing has echoed his hopes, fears, and aspirations and, above all, his enduring, passionate love for his wife Elsa.

Louis Aragon was born on October 3, 1897 in Paris in the elegant sixteenth district, the "Beaux Quartiers" which lend their name to the title of one of his novels. His family ran a pension which he was later to depict in two of his novels. At the age of eleven, he received as a prize for scholastic excellence a book entitled *Vingt-cinq années de vie littéraire*. He subsequently described this anthology of selections from the work of Maurice Barrès as a revelation that determined the orientation of his life.[2] The sheer physical beauty of Barrès' language influenced Aragon's decision to become a writer.[3] From Barrès, as well as from Stendhal, he learned the message of lyrical individualism and the search for happiness through the egotistical cultivation of one's own sensations. This process of introspection was to be employed in his Surrealist period. Later on, as his concept of the role of the artist changed, Aragon was to see in Stendhal, not the methodical egotist, but the representative of critical realism, working for the transformation of society.

Aragon discovered in his early childhood the world of books. In *J'Abats mon jeu* (*I Lay my Cards on the Table*), Aragon wrote that he had spent half of his life reading and that, if he had not read so much, he would not have written as much. André Breton wrote that as early as 1919, Aragon had in truth read everything.[4] It was Aragon's mother who introduced him to the great Russian writers, but when she surprised him reading a book by the Communist Maxim Gorky, she took it away, exclaiming that Gorky was not for him. "That must have been in 1907, and I remained convinced that Maxim Gorky was a rather risqué writer."[5] Two years later, a young Georgian woman, a guest in their pension who was to serve as a model for his Catherine Simonidzé (*Les Cloches de Bâle*), gave him Gorky to read. "That my mother had forbidden me to read his works two years earlier dumbfounded me: what was there in these books other than the most elevated, pure, and noble sentiments? Why had I been forbidden to read them? Was my family on the side of those who were evil? The matter seemed so strange to me, and of such grave consequence, that I told no one about what I was reading."[6]

Although he stopped believing in God soon after his first communion, Aragon writes that there remained within his soul a certain unused religious ardor. And it was Gorky who gave direction to this ardor. He has said that each rereading of the works of Gorky awakens within him the same emotions he felt as a child, as well as echoes of his youthful uncertainties and hopes. In his writing, Aragon has sought to achieve the tone of Gorky, which he describes as the "quivering of life."[7]

After having completed his secondary studies at the Lycée Carnot in Paris in 1916, Aragon passed his baccalaureat examinations and enrolled in the preparatory year for medical studies. In a long autobiographical poem, *Le Roman inachevé*, Aragon, writing of the period of World War I, spoke of these medical studies. "And when they were dying at Vimy/*I* was learning about anatomy."[8] In 1917, he entered the army as a medical aide, an experience he also described in *Le Roman inachevé*: "I had my twentieth birthday in the barracks/Thin child dressed in blue/Dreaming much and eating little."[9] At Val-de-Grâce, he met André Breton, who was also serving in the medical corps, and Philippe Soupault. This meeting was to prove of great significance in the history of the Surrealist movement. Aragon took part in the last operations of the war, for which he was awarded the Croix de guerre, and then participated in the occupation of the Saar and the Rhineland. In his novel *La Semaine sainte* (*Holy Week*) of 1958, Aragon described an experience he had at that time which was to weigh heavily in his destiny. He was twenty-two years old. His unit was stationed near Saarbrücken. The year was 1919 and there had been strikes in the mines. The miners feared to go down into the mines because of dangerous conditions. The men of Aragon's infantry battalion were mounting guard under orders to shoot the miners unless they returned to the pits. Suddenly, Aragon realized that it was the miners who were right, that their resistance expressed "everything that was great and noble in man."[10] It was to this experience that the author attributes the awakening of his social conscience

Aragon prided himself on the fact that there was no mention of the war in his postwar works. This represented a refusal to grant reality to so repugnant an institution. Eleven years later, in his *Traité du style*, Aragon was to write about his disgust for this "revolting institution." He maintained that he would never again wear the French uniform, "the livery they threw upon my shoulders eleven years ago."[11] His refusal to be classified as a war veteran is expressed in the poem "Ancien combattant," in which he mocks those who would forever remain bound by former classifications: "I took part in the Dada movement/Said the Dadaist/And in truth/He Had."[12]

II *Dada to Surrealism*

Upon his return to Paris, Aragon collaborated with André Breton and Philippe Soupault on a review, *Littérature*, which was devoted to avant-garde poetry. The first edition of the magazine contained some of Aragon's poems which were to appear later in *Feu de joie* (1920). This group subsequently became affiliated with the Dadaists led by Tristan Tzara. February 1916 is usually given as the birthdate in Zurich of the Dada movement, but similar movements were already under way in Paris and New York. However, it was in Zurich that the movement was baptized. Opening a dictionary at random, Tzara came upon the word "dada," meaning a child's hobbyhorse or a pet subject, a name he promptly adopted. Aragon and his friends were drawn to the Dada movement which represented an attempt to destroy traditional values, both in life and in art. They participated in the demonstrations of the Dadaists to shock the traditional enemy, the bourgeoisie. The purely negative nature of the group is evident in the following manifesto by Aragon:

No more painters, no more writers, no more musicians, no more sculptors, no more religions, no more republicans, no more royalists, no more imperialists, no more anarchists, no more socialists, no more Bolsheviks, no more politicians, no more proletarians, no more democrats, no more armies, no more police, no more nations, no more of these idiocies, no more, no more, NOTHING, NOTHING, NOTHING.[13]

Gradually the *Littérature* group turned away from the sterility of Dada and moved toward Surrealism. In *Pour un réalisme socialiste* (*For Socialist Realism*), Aragon wrote that Surrealism was a desperate effort to go beyond the negation of Dada and to reconstruct a new reality.[14] This desire to rebuild the world to ensure a better life for man has been one of the basic themes in Aragon's work.

The discoveries of Einstein and Freud had revealed at this time the possibilities of totally new patterns of thought. Under the influence of Freud, Breton and his group became preoccupied with the potentialities of the human subconscious as a source of artistic inspiration. To plunge into this source, they employed automatic writing. This was described by André Breton as "pure psychic automatism, by which an attempt is made to express, either orally, or in writing, or in any other manner, the true functioning of thought. The dictation of thought, in the absence of all control by the reason, excluding any esthetic or moral preoccupation."[15] It was only by this process of free association that the artist might receive a revelation of the basic truths about himself. In a section of *Le Roman inachevé* entitled "Words Took Me by the Hand," Aragon spoke of those moments of automatic writing when three or four of them sat together at the end of the day "marrying sounds" to rebuild the world.[16]

Recitations of dreams were as valuable as free association, since the subconscious mind was unconstrained while the individual was asleep. The Surrealists were content to transcribe the images that had been formed by dreams and free association without seeking to interpret them. Art, in their opinion, should only transmit the image without attempting to elicit proofs from it. The words which they transcribed expressed the true sensations and experiences of the poet.

Although they concentrated mainly on the subconscious mind and its manifestations, the Surrealists did not ignore conscious reality. Their poetic goal was the fusion of dreams and reality into a single entity, which was to be the absolute reality, or *sur-réalité* (super-reality). Thus it was their poetry, combining the thinkable with the unthinkable, and written presumably with the help of some force outside themselves, that was to uncover truth and knowledge for them. "We were great, grown children, passionate and honest, revolted by all pretense, all complacency, madly exacting for ourselves and for the world,"[17] wrote Aragon.

Woman, as well as poetry, represented a means of communication with the marvelous. Through the intermediary of love, the Surrealists felt that man entered into communion with the forces of the imagination lying within the subconscious mind. Love became the doorway to the absolute. The Surrealists, influenced by Freud's teaching that the libido was the chief factor motivating man's acts and thoughts, preached total sexual liberation. In practice, however, love took on for them the form of an exclusive passion. Through their constant devotion to a single woman, they hoped to facilitate communication with the absolute and achieve new insights into themselves.

In *Le Paysan de Paris* (*The Peasant of Paris*), Aragon wrote that love was at the source of the metaphysical state of mind and that he no longer wanted to leave what he called its "enchanted forest."[18] In the same work, he defined love as a state of confusion of the real and of the marvelous, proclaiming that it was time to set up the religion of love.[19] All of Aragon's subsequent collections of love poetry, culminating in *Le Fou d'Elsa*, were devoted to establishing this religion of love. The Surrealist cult of the mythical woman became, in Aragon's post-Surrealist work, the cult of a real woman, his wife Elsa, who was the source of and inspiration for most of his work after 1928. While, in his Surrealist period, love was an opening into the world of the marvelous, the love of Elsa provided for Aragon an entry into the real world "in which it was worthwhile to live and to die."[20] Love was no longer a mystical participation, but the finding of another and, through the other, the discovery of the rest of humanity. From Elsa, Aragon learned that the love dreamed of by the Surrealists could take tangible shape in this world. However, it was the Surrealist attitude toward love that had prepared Aragon for this exclusive passion. In *Le Cahier noir*, an extract from an unpublished novel, *Défense de l'infini*, Aragon described his receptivity to love:

Thus, completely possessed by the idea of love, I assured myself that I would love one day. I felt within me the possibility, even the fatality of passion . . . . *I am going to love* . . . A man thus dissolves. He no longer has a separate life. He is invaded by a woman as if by a perfume. Little by little, this woman becomes identified with his most subliminal thoughts. He carries within him an echo of her . . . . The desire for love prepares and engenders love. You must want to love . . . . An idea of perfection is certainly hidden for me in the depths of the concept of love . . . . This cult fills my entire life . . . . Thus did I spend the years of my youth between idleness and sensuality, awaiting an abstract love.[21]

III   *Surrealism to Communism*

In *Littératures soviétiques*, Aragon described his meeting with Elsa Triolet and with her brother-in-law, the Russian poet Mayakovsky, both of whom were to reveal to him the overwhelming reality of Soviet Russia. On November 28, 1928, in an enormous café in Montparnasse, a stranger at an adjoining table extended an invitation to Aragon on behalf of Mayakovsky to sit at his table. Aragon accepted and sat down beside him "with all this romanticism in my heart, and the dizzying Parisian ignorance. I did not know that as a result of this, my life was going to change completely. And the next day, in the same drafty, disordered place . . . I met Elsa Triolet. We have never been apart since then."[22] The role played by Elsa in the life and work of Aragon has been incalculable, first as initiator to the Soviet revolution and Soviet literature, and then as a guide leading him to a new concept of the social mission of the writer. It is his love for Elsa that has inspired Aragon's most beautiful poetry. Their marriage has been the model for the couple he has proposed as the cornerstone of an ideal society of the future. "I still did not understand that it was possible for a woman to sum up for me human relationships and shed light on them, and that, through her, I would henceforth understand what was worthwhile and what was not."[23] It was Mayakovsky who revealed to Aragon that the mission of the writer was to contribute by his work to the establishment of a better world. Aragon wrote in *Pour un réalisme socialiste* that Mayakovksy, who had known how to make an arm of poetry, was to be the link that joined him to the new world.[24]

Even before his meeting with Elsa and Mayakovsky, Aragon, like the other Surrealists, had been attracted to the Russian revolution which echoed their hatred of bourgeois society. After publication of the first *Surrealist Manifesto*, the title of the magazine *Littérature* had been changed to *La Révolution surréaliste*. The Surrealists now declared that their movement was more than an artistic movement. In order to change life, as Rimbaud had counseled, it was necessary to follow the precepts of Marx and transform the world. The first issue of *La Révolution surréaliste* appeared in 1923. Later on, in keeping with their changing goals, they changed the title to *Le Surréalisme au service de la révolution*.

Surrealism had existed originally in a political vacuum. The revolt of the Surrealists against society had not been based on an interest in any political philosophy. Aragon made this clear in a letter to Jean Bernier, the editor of the Communist magazine *Clarté*, when he stated that he placed the spirit of revolt far above any politics. As for the Russian revolution, he continued, "forgive me for shrugging my shoulders. On the level of ideas, it is, at best, a vague ministerial crisis."[25] Although both the Communists and the Surrealists advocated destruction of the existing social structure, the revolution envisaged by the Surrealists was mainly in the domain of ideas. They wanted to free the imagination from the inhibitions placed upon it by centuries of culture and laws. They believed that once the imagination had been liberated and complete freedom of expression was permitted, a perfect society would automatically ensue. "Everything stems from the imagination, and everything is revealed by it,"[26] wrote Aragon. Thus, initially, the inhibitions placed upon the individual by a Communistic society were as repugnant to the Surrealists as those under which they were living. Their perfect society was a state of anarchy. As long as the artist had complete freedom, moral considerations, including the obligations of the individual to society, were unimportant.

Gradually the Surrealists realized that a revolution in the field of ideas was impossible without a complete revamping of the social structure. Since pure anarchy was sterile, Aragon and many of the Surrealists were obliged to ally themselves with a group which, while working toward a practicable goal, could give meaning to their revolt. Thus, they turned more and more towards the Communists. The turning point in the relationship between the Surrealists and the Communists was the Moroccan War of 1925. The crisis was set off by the rebellion in the Riff against the French. The leader Abd-el-Krim had been encouraged to embark upon a general offensive against foreign occupation after defeating the Spanish army in 1921. Pétain was sent to quell the insurrection and, in 1926, a joint Spanish-French army ended the rebellion. Before that, in November 1925, one hundred and five French Communist militants were imprisoned for their active opposition to the Moroccan War. The Surrealists, whose initial revolt had been motivated by the horrors of World War I, now saw war recur, but this time against a colonial people seeking its freedom. They joined with the Communists in condemning the war, which Aragon was later to decry in the poem "Front Rouge": "Listen to the cry of the Syrians killed by aerial darts/by the aviators of the Third Republic/Hear the groans of the dying Moroccans . . . ."[27] Their agreement was further confirmed in a manifesto, *La Révolution d'abord et toujours*, in which they stressed the social nature of true revolution. Before a revolution in the field of ideas could be attempted, it was necessary to change the physical order of things.

As early as 1920, Aragon, overwhelmed by the visions of a new world revealed at the Tours Congress of the Socialist Party, applied for membership in the newly founded Communist Party. Georges Pioch, at that time secretary of the Seine Federation, was skeptical of Aragon's reliability and turned him away. Aragon persisted in his interest and, together with Breton, Eluard, and some lesser Surrealist writers, joined the Communist Party in 1927. In 1930, Aragon participated in the Congress of Revolutionary Writers in Kharkov and, upon his return, published in an issue of the Surrealist publication, *Le Surréalisme au service de la révolution*, an article entitled "Le surréalisme et le devenir révolutionnaire." This was his final attempt to maintain his autonomy as a Surrealist while recognizing the common interest of the Surrealist and Communist movements. He has since described that article as "a desperate attempt, the last, to reconcile the attitude that had been mine for years and the new reality with which I came into contact."[28] However, Aragon's definitive break with the Surrealists did not come until after the incident that has since been named the "Aragon Affair."

While in Russia, Aragon wrote a long revolutionary poem called "Front Rouge" ("Red Front"), in which he attacked the French government and called for the murder of its leaders: "I sing the violent domination of the bourgeoisie/by the Proletariat/for the annihilation of this bourgeoisie/for the total annihilation of this bourgeoisie."[29] He called upon his comrades to: "Fire on Léon Blum/Fire on Boncour Frossard Déat/Fire on the trained bears of social democracy."[30]

As a result of this work, Aragon was convicted in January, 1932 of inciting soldiers to mutiny and of provocation to murder and was given a suspended five-year prison sentence. André Breton and the Surrealists came to Aragon's defense with a petition called "Misère de la poésie," in which they protested against any attempt to interpret a poetic text for what they termed judicial ends. In keeping with the Surrealist esthetic, they maintained that the poet is merely the interpreter of subjective and objective reality and, as such, is not responsible for his writings. As for the poem itself, Breton admitted that he did not like it. Such a form of poetry seemed to him to be a step backward:

Front Rouge does not open a new path for poetry; it would be futile to propose it to today's poets as an example, for the excellent reason that in such a domain an objective point of departure can be only an objective point of arrival, and that, in this poem, we find the *return to the external subject* and especially to the *emotional subject* . . . [31]

Aragon disavowed their defense and broke definitively with the Surrealists, a break which they interpreted as a betrayal. Despite the bitterness between Aragon and the Surrealists occasioned by this rupture, many years later, in his autobiographical poem *Le Roman inachevé*, he defended the movement:

> Despite all that separated us
> Oh my friends of that time
> It is you whom I see again
>
> . . . .
>
> We shared our dawn like a loaf of bread
> It was after all a marvelous spring[32]

Although life separated him from many of these early companions and set them against each other, Aragon wrote: "I swear that at the beginning it was like pure water."[33]

Surrealism left an indelible imprint on the work of Aragon. In the collection of essays *J'Abats mon jeu*, he wrote that he had studied all of his life to become the man he is, but that he has never forgotten the man or men he was, for they were stages that led to what he is now. The Surrealist dissatisfaction with the world about them and their desire to transform life are reflected throughout Aragon's work. Their concept of literature as a force for the liberation of man was to remain Aragon's concept of literature, whether Surrealist, Resistance or Communist. Their search for an absolute has been Aragon's lifelong search, and their concept of woman as the bearer of magical powers leading to the conquest of this absolute has led to the rehabilitation of woman and to the subsequent concept of the couple as the base of a new society. Paul Eluard, an early Surrealist and one of the finest poets of the twentieth century, expressed this idea of personal love leading to communion with the rest of mankind when he wrote:

> We will not go to the goal one by one but by twos
> Knowing ourselves by twos we will all know each
>   other
> We will all love one another and our children
>   will laugh
> At the black legend in which a solitary man cries[34]

IV *Toward "Singing Tomorrows"*

After the publication of "Front Rouge" and his rupture with the Surrealists, Aragon wrote that the only action worthy of a man and of a poet was to sing the glory of the new world of Communism.[35] All of his activity until the advent of World War II was to further the cause of Communism. Aragon pursued his goal on several levels, as a poet, journalist, novelist, and militant. In 1935, he stood up against the threat of a Fascist putsch in France in his role as one of the Secretaries of the Association of Writers for the Defense of Culture. In 1936, he received the Théophraste-Renaudot prize for his novel *Les Beaux Quartiers*, a novel belonging to a series that was to reveal the corrupt bourgeois world crumbling away to make way for a future in which books would be written "for peaceful men who are masters of their own destiny."[36] From 1937 on, Aragon was co-director of the Communist newspaper *Ce Soir*, a post he occupied until the paper was suppressed during the turbulent period of the Nazi-Soviet pact under orders of the French government. While this pact alienated many French intellectuals from the Communist Party, Aragon, in his editorials, maintained that the Franco-Soviet pact remained valid despite Russia's new alliance and that Paris and London should hasten to reach an agreement with Moscow. While Aragon and other party intellectuals remained loyal to the party, many of their idealistic friends were outraged at the pact between the Soviet leaders and the Nazis, who were at that moment threatening the freedom of Poland. Paul Nizan, one of the more prominent Communist intellectuals, had echoed Aragon's demand for a Franco-Soviet rapprochement after the signing of the pact. After he was drafted, he realized that the interests of Russia no longer coincided with the national interests of France, and resigned from the party. After Nizan died at Dunkirk, he was subjected to a campaign of vilification by the Communist Party which regarded his resignation as an act of treason. In *Les Communistes* (1949), Aragon depicted Nizan as the treacherous Patrice Orfilat, a coward who, when he sees the war approaching, decides to save himself by securing a job with the government. All of the events of these years were transcribed into this vast novel whose major thesis was that the French government was more interested in the suppression of the Communists than in combatting fascism.

V *Poet of France*

Mobilized in 1939, Aragon served as an "auxiliary doctor" with warrant officer rank, first in a regiment of Czechoslovakian and Spanish refugees and then in a light motorized division. Evacuated from Dunkirk, his division returned to France and fought on the Lower Seine. Taken prisoner at Angoulême, Aragon escaped with thirty men. He received the Croix de guerre twice and the Médaille Militaire. Not only Aragon, but the majority of French Communists remained loyally at their posts, despite their attempts to rationalize the Nazi-Soviet pact, and fought bravely for France until her defeat.

During the years of the German occupation of France, Aragon devoted himself to the task of keeping alive the spirit of freedom among his countrymen. He exhorted all Frenchmen to take heart and to fight against their oppressors. It has been said that his love for his country finally permitted him to fulfill his true role, that of a great French traditional writer.[37] Aragon became a symbol of resistance both in France and abroad, and tribute was paid to him in many countries. The six collections of poetry he wrote during the years of the war run the gamut of wartime emotions, from the first bitterness and distress to the joy of liberation. His prose writings of the period appeared in many clandestine publications under numerous pseudonyms, the most famous of which was François la Colère (François the Wrathful) and were united in the postwar collection

Servitude et Grandeur des Français and the two volumes of *L'Homme Communiste*.

Aragon wanted his message to reach the greatest possible number of Frenchmen and, to secure wide popularity for his poems, he employed devices such as frequent use of local color and constant references to places and things familiar to all his compatriots. Many of these poems contained the musical simplicity of the old ballads and could often be sung. Aragon wanted to restore poetry to the important place it had occupied during the days of the troubadours of the twelfth century. Unlike his early Surrealist poetry which had been directed toward a select few, the wartime poetry of Aragon was written for the masses.

VI *Aragon, French Communist*

After the Liberation, Aragon again devoted himself to his party. In 1947, he became director of the revived *Ce Soir* and, in 1948, was deprived of his civil rights for ten years as a result of an editorial in this paper. In 1949, he joined the staff of the newspaper *Les Lettres Françaises* and became its director in 1953 after the demise of *Ce Soir*. He was elected to membership on the Central Committee of the French Communist Party in 1950 and received the Lenin Peace Prize in 1957. Despite his considerable involvement in political affairs, Aragon's literary activity since the war has been vast and diverse, including journalism, novels, poetry, and art criticism. To give the French reader a curiosity and taste for Russian literature, Aragon established in the 1950s a program with Gallimard for the translation and publication of contemporary Russian works. He has written many prefaces to these works and translated the love story *Djamilia* by Aitmatov. In 1955, he published *Littératures soviétiques* and, in 1956, *Introduction aux littératures soviétiques*. The titles are written in the plural to point out the multiplicity of peoples of the Soviet Union whose divergent traditions had led them to a common destiny. One of the major goals of these works was to dispel the misconception shared by both Communists and non-Communists that Russian literature came directly out of the Revolution and had no connection with what preceded it. On the contrary, Soviet literature is the direct offspring of Russian literature; Soviet realism is the result of a long past marked by such names as Gogol, Tolstoy, Dostoevsky, and Gorky.

In 1963, Aragon collaborated with André Maurois on a four-volume *Histoire parallèle (U.R.S.S.–U.S.A.)*. Aragon wrote the two volumes on Soviet history, Maurois one on United States history, and the fourth volume contained interviews with important Russians and Americans. The unifying element between the two histories is the idea that both countries started their modern existence in 1917, the Soviet Union with the Revolution and the United States with its entry into World War I and its subsequent involvement in European affairs. Aragon's work is in a sense a news encyclopedia of events in Russia from 1917 to 1960, reported from the perspective of a faithful party member.

Aragon did not join with other French intellectuals in condemning the Russian intervention in Hungary and their overthrow of the Nagy government. However, on November 8, 1956, the Directing Committee of the National Committee of Writers, consisting both of Communist members like Aragon and non-Communists like Sartre, publicly called on Kádár, the Hungarian Communist leader, to protect the physical and moral interests of Hungarian writers. They also added that the committee was profoundly divided over the meaning of recent events in Hungary. It was the Soviet trial of the writers Sinyavsky and Daniel that finally brought Aragon to speak out and he denounced the trial for establishing criminality of opinion, a precedent which he described as more injurious to the interests of socialism than the works of these writers could possibly be.

Soviet leaders, unable to forgive Aragon for his attitude in the writer's trial and for his refusal to attend the fourth Writers' Congress and the 1967 celebrations of the revolution, decided to attack him through Lili Brick, Elsa's sister, whom they have denounced as having exerted a nefarious influence on Vladimir Mayakovsky. The final revelation that Soviet interests did not coincide necessarily with French interests came with the 1968 invasion of Czechoslovakia, an invasion which Aragon condemned in unison with the entire French Communist Party. While he has repudiated Soviet aggression, he has not repudiated communism. But the pendulum has swung back again from the "International" to the "Marseillaise." French interests again take precedence. In 1955, Aragon wrote that when asked whether he is primarily a Communist or a writer, he answers that he is first of all a writer and that is why he is a Communist.[38] His most recent works testify to the fact that he is indeed primarily a writer, one who claims the right to forsake militancy at times to "dream a bit at the turning of the road."[39] With each passing year, he writes with increasing speed, impelled by the knowledge that: "One day I will die without having said all/Those moments of happiness those burning noons/The immense black night with golden streaks."[40] Since 1960, Aragon's works have combined the subjective idealism of his early Surrealist works with the Socialist Realism of the subsequent texts. He has described his evolution as a man and as a writer in the following words:

I have not always been the man I am. I have learned all my life in order to become the man I am, but I have not forgotten the man I was, or rather the men I have been. And if, between these men and me there is a contradiction, I think that I have learned and progressed while changing. These men, when I turn to look at them, do not make me ashamed, they are the stages of what I am, they led to me, I cannot say *Me* without them. . . . I do not have a single certainty that came to me other than through doubt, anguish, sweat, pain of the experience.[41]

CHAPTER 2

In Search of an Absolute—
From Surrealism to Communism

I Feu de joie

"Down with the world, I will make it more beautiful,"[1] cried Louis
Aragon in his first published work, *Feu de joie* (*Bonfire*) of 1920. This
small volume contained twenty-five poems, many of which had already
appeared in magazines. His desire to "Break this universe over the bent
knee/Dry wood which would make remarkable flames,"[2] echoes the
proposal of the Dadaists to destroy all traditional institutions and values.
Despite the absolute nihilism of Dada, Aragon spares certain aspects of life
in his *tabula rasa*. Certain positive themes which appear in his work of this
early period continue to reappear throughout his work. In protest against
the ugliness of war and life, he sings of the joys of childhood and
adolescence with their discoveries, hesitations, and purity. He expresses in
Feu de joie a nostalgia for childhood and school and for the marvelous
times when school was out: "As a schoolboy I held Sundays/like a balloon
in my two hands/On the day of the circus and friends/Friends/Apples and
peaches/under their caps in the English style."[3] He evokes the great heat
of summer vacations at the end of the school year and the countryside
lying somnolently "on the fringes of time."[4] There is also faith in beauty
"the only virtue who still stretches forth her pure hands."[5] Paris, the
Seine, and the marvels of everyday life, which were to constitute the
modern mythology for the Surrealists, also appear in this collection: "The
Seine dances in the April sun/Like Cécile at her first ball."[6] The poem
"Fugue" reveals Aragon's eternal preoccupation with love, here envisaged
as the fruit of seductiveness and charm: "Turn heads, turn laughs/For the
love of whom/For the love of me/For the love of me."[7] A few years later,
he wrote: "It seems that I am seduction personified,"[8] a view corrobo-
rated by André Breton in his memoirs where he described Aragon as a man
of inordinate charm.

II Le Mouvement perpétuel

This collection, published in 1926, includes poems written by Aragon
from 1920 to 1924. The "Perpetual Movement" referred to in the title

symbolizes the continual effort required to go beyond and surpass oneself: "Are you going to drag out your whole life amid the throng/Half dead/ Half asleep/Haven't you had enough of platitudes."[9] Defiance of the bourgeoisie is expressed in the dedication of the book: "I dedicate this book to Poetry/And —— on those who read it," as well as in poems like "Persiennes" in which Aragon merely repeats the word "Venetian blinds" twenty times. The poem "Suicide," which consists of a simple recital of the alphabet, illustrates the belief of the Surrealists that traditional use of language was a form of artistic suicide. Another poem, "Sommeil de plomb" ("Leaden Sleep"), describes the hypnotic trances cultivated by the Surrealists in their effort to explore the dark, mysterious country hidden within the recesses of the mind. In "Une Vague de rêves" ("A Wave of Dreams"), Aragon mentioned that an epidemic of trances broke out among the Surrealists. "There were some seven or eight who now lived only for those moments of oblivion when, with the lights out, they spoke without consciousness, like drowned men in the open air . . . ."[10] Some, like Robert Desnos, could dispense with any preliminary steps and fall asleep at will:

"In a café, amid the sound of voices, the bright light, the jostlings, Robert Desnos need only close his eyes, and he talks, and among the steins, the saucers, the whole ocean collapses with its prophetic racket and its vapors decorated with long oriflammes However little those who interrogate this amazing sleeper incite him, prophecy, the tone of magic, of revelation, of revolution, the tone of the fanatic and the apostle, immediately appear. Under other conditions, Desnos, were he to cling to this delirium, would become the leader of a religion. . . ."[11]

And always, it was the image that could reveal this "subterranean world of dreams."[12] In the *Surrealist Manifesto*, André Breton described the power of the image:

There is no alternative but to admit that the two terms of the image . . . are simultaneous products of the activity I call surrealist, reason confining itself to noting and appreciating the luminous phenomenon . . . One might even say that the images appear, in the dizzying race, to be the only guidons of the intelligence. The mind becomes convinced little by little of the supreme reality of these images.[13]

The Surrealists believed that the power of the image could be attributed to the fact that words had their own existence. For them, words were objects: "Pass me the word/Thank you/I have the key/The bolt begins to move like a tongue."[14] In "Une Vague de rêves," the first manifesto of his poetic generation, Aragon wrote that thoughts could not exist except as they were embodied in words. He also described in this work the mental activity which produced these images: "Sometimes, I suddenly lose the whole thread of my life. . . . For this moment in which everything eludes me, in which immense cracks appear in the palace of the world, I would sacrifice all my life if, at that price, it could be made to last."[15] He told how the first Surrealists would meet together at night as if after a day's shooting to draw up an account of the day's sport, of the fantastic plants and beasts they had invented, and of the images they had bagged. They spent an increasing amount of time at this pursuit, the numbers of images increased and took on the characteristics of visual, auditory, and tactile hallucinations. Gradually, the poets lost the power to govern these hallucinations and, instead, became their slaves.

While many of the images in *Le Mouvement perpétuel* may have been the product of automatic writing, the majority suggest a conscious artistry at work. Even though poems in free verse predominate, there are poems in regular verse in this collection, including a sonnet, "Un Air embaumé," written in rich rhyme and dedicated to Guillaume Apollinaire, the father of Surrealism. In 1947, in a theoretical work on poetry, entitled "De l'exactitude historique en poésie," Aragon revealed that his poetry from the outset had been the result of conscious effort. Stating that he preferred the designations counted and uncounted to free and regular verse, Aragon maintained that he had written counted verse all his life, because all free verse is merely a combination of verses in varying meters, each of which is in fact counted.[16]

In his *Traité du style*, Aragon gave the following definition of Surrealism to show that it was not a refuge against style:

Surrealism is inspiration recognized, accepted and practiced. No longer as an inexplicable visitation, but as a faculty that is exercised. Normally limited by fatigue. Of a variable scope, depending on individual forces. And the results of which are of unequal interest.[17]

Content and form were of prime importance in Surrealist works, although not in the traditional sense. "There is a legend that it is enough to learn the trick and that immediately texts of great poetic interest will flow from the pen of anyone at all," Aragon wrote in the same work. Because these poets did not labor over their poems did not mean that they were badly written. "Who has told you that to write well, one must stop for seven years between each word. Writing well is like walking straight."[18] And content was of equal importance since it gave to the text its power of revelation. Although the artist did not know beforehand what he was going to write, and although what he had written, upon rereading, did not seem familiar, this did not by any means signify that what he had written was of little consequence. It was only when he wrote a letter or something similar that he produced trivia, since there his will and reason had intervened to prevent free expression. Thus, Aragon concluded, far from being easy to write, Surrealist poetry was the most difficult of all to produce because in Surrealism the poet was bound by strict laws. The rigorous discipline to which he was obliged to submit was based on the use of language, on words and their meanings in the Surrealist rather than in the dictionary sense. The true meaning of words was to be found in their every letter and syllable.

III   Anicet ou le Panorama roman

Anicet or the Panorama Novel (1921) is the first of Aragon's prose works of this period. It is both a picaresque story and a philosophical tale. It represents an attempt to define the revolt of the young generation and to denounce the illusion and hypocrisy of traditional systems and solutions. Aragon started this work at the front and completed it two years later. While it ridicules the usual technique of the novel and its descriptions, logical sequences of events, and development of character, it is still a narrative, written in defiance of both the Surrealists and the Dadaists who condemned the novel as a literary form. Aragon underlined his rebellion by inserting the word "roman" ("novel") as the last word of the title.

The book opens in the manner of a Voltairian tale as the author introduces the hero, Anicet, who has retained from his secondary studies only the rule of the three dramatic unities and the concept of the relativity of time and space. These represent the extent of his knowledge of art and of life. Because of his unorthodox behavior, Anicet's parents realized that he was a poet and sent him on the trip that was to be his introduction to poetry and to life. He arrives at an inn and sees a man at an adjoining table who leaves his food untouched, yet who seems to be experiencing all the gastronomic pleasures of a gourmet. Anicet realizes by this behavior that this man is a free spirit and enters into conversation with him. He learns that he is the poet Rimbaud, whom he has always admired for his contribution to poetry. In his discussion with Rimbaud, Anicet attacks those poets who have followed Rimbaud blindly and who, by their slavish imitation, have ignored the poet's basic message of personal liberty. Rimbaud's teachings are compared to a woman, the personification of beauty and the ideal of Rimbaud's contemporaries. Anicet tells Rimbaud that, when he left this "woman" to realize his personal destiny, "she increasingly made herself more available to all as her charms faded. For a moment she was able to hold me . . . . But when I saw the outdated philtres she was using, I did not persist in my error and left in search of the modern idea of life."[19]

From Rimbaud, the young Anicet learns the supreme goal of life, love. He teaches the boy the religion of love, a religion Aragon has faithfully practiced throughout his life. When he describes life with his beloved, he says: "Existence with her did not have love as a goal, it was love itself."[20] And later, using words that anticipate Aragon's future words to Elsa, he adds: "It is only in the narrative that I use the personal pronoun in the first person plural when speaking about us. We were only a single person, a single will, a single love."[21]

When the poet has finished speaking, Anicet, in the manner of a hero of an eighteenth-century novel, replies with the story of his life. This story is distinguished from Aragon's previous works, for it contains the urban magic discovered by the Surrealists, the new poetic force existing in automobiles, machines, and other elements of contemporary life. In a description which anticipates his famous account of the "Passage de l'Opéra" in *Le Paysan de Paris*, Aragon evokes one of the covered arcades which formerly existed in Paris and which were filled with mystery and adventure for the Surrealists. Among the shops in the arcade through which Anicet passed daily were those of a wallpaper dealer, a grocer who sold exotic foods, two tailors, and a shop selling orthopedic devices. "Décor which delights my sensibility, I baptize you Arcade of Cosmoràmas . . . where everything offers itself to me so that I may transform life in my own way."[22] As fantastic shapes began to take form before his eyes, Anicet would tell himself in vain that he was prey to illusions, that the scratching of the nails of the jackals on the dead leaves, the howling of the white wolves, and the hissing of the boa constrictors were nothing more than the noise of the sewing machines. In vain would he tell himself that he ran no danger, terror still would take hold of him by means of his imagination.[23]

In the course of his search for the meaning of life, a metaphysical quest that is apparent in all of Aragon's work, Anicet is initiated into a secret society, the members of which are devoted to the cult of a certain Mirabelle, who symbolizes both woman and modern beauty. "One might almost believe that Mire follows her worshipers, watches them, listens to them and that, when they speak or act to her liking, this beauty appears to them in recognition of their merits."[24] The seven members of this secret society represent André Breton, Jean Cocteau, Charlie Chaplin, Paul Valéry, Picasso, Jacques Vaché, and a combination of Max Jacob and Reverdy. Each member, vying for her favor, brings offerings to Mirabelle which express the esthetics of the donor. Of all of the gifts, Anicet prefers the one of Max Jacob (Chipre) because of its intimate bond between esthetics and ethics: "What constituted Chipre's authority in his eyes was that his esthetics were so marvelously adapted to his life that he moved without realizing it from considerations on life to considerations on art. Truly one could be certain that his esthetics were his moral code."[25]

To become a member of the secret society, Anicet must perform an act to prove himself to his fellow members, who can only judge his esthetics by his actions. His first act of hommage to Mirabelle is a destructive one; he breaks into museums, steals those paintings that represent the art of the past, and burns them on top of the Arc de Triomphe. He eliminates what was formerly considered beautiful to make way for true modern beauty. After he is accepted into the society, he continues to question his fellow members, still seeking the way in which "to systematize life."[26] From Picasso (Bleu), he learns that "art is only a form of love: that appears evident in the dance, from which flow the plastic arts, and in song, from which flow music and the literary arts. I have never painted except to seduce," concludes Bleu.[27] When he compares himself to Bleu, Anicet feels that he is unable to compete because of the basic superiority of the painter's medium. It was easy to explain the painter's power of fascination. "How is it possible not to love the one who gives us at every instant the human equivalent of external things? Poor poet who seeks to compete with his miserable verbal images."[28]

From André Breton (Baptiste Ajamais), he learns that the conquest of Mirabelle is only an episode, the first step in his life toward a mysterious goal. And then a mysterious voice whispers to him a message that has never varied in Aragon's work:

Love is your last chance. . . . There is really nothing else on earth to hold you . . . the experience of others is worth nothing to you . . . Note that in an era when one can, without unleashing a storm, deny God, Home and Country, one would have his eyes torn out if he declared that art does not exist. Art and Beauty are man's last divinities. They commit that singular error of considering Mire to be Beauty, while . . . in reality, she is woman. Truly Anicet, Woman is your last chance of salvation. To conquer her, you must fight, to keep her you must fight; that is an interest you can still take in life. If that is not enough for you, my dear friend, you may as well throw in the sponge.[29]

IV Les Aventures de Télémaque

When this work appeared in 1922, the rupture between the Dadaists and the Surrealists had occurred. Aragon and his friends had turned against the complete sterility of Dada. Aragon has declared that *Les Aventures de Télémaque* represented a compromise he made with the Surrealists who condemned the novel as a literary form. He effected this compromise by incorporating into the story, in the guise of speeches by the protagonists, manifestoes that he had written earlier. Thus the work became both the affirmation and the negation of the novel.

Télémaque's speech affirming the belief of the Surrealists in the independent existence of words was taken from one of twenty-three manifestoes published in issue number thirteen of the magazine *Littérature*: "Everything that is not me is incomprehensible. . . . Language, no matter how else it may seem, is reduced to me alone, and if I repeat any word at all, that word sheds everything that is not me until it becomes an organic sound by means of which my life reveals itself."[30]

Les Aventures de Télémaque continues the theme of the search already found in *Anicet*. The title, plot, and characters are borrowed from Fénélon's prose epic poem of the seventeenth century, but the message of Aragon's work is the message of anarchy. Télémaque, the son of Ulysses, accompanied by his tutor, Mentor, lands on the island of Ogyvie where he has come in search of his father. There he is tempted by two women, the goddess Calypso and the nymph Eucharis. Each development of the story elicits moral reflections on the part of Mentor, but while the Mentor of Fénélon taught a moral lesson, Aragon's Mentor preaches a Dadaist nihilism:

The System D makes you free; break everything . . . . You are the masters of everything you break. You were given laws, morals, esthetics to make you respect fragile things. What is fragile should be broken. Test your strength once; after that I defy you not to continue. What you cannot break will break you, will be your master.[31]

But the sterile message of Mentor's system can no longer satisfy Télémaque. To refute the arguments of his preceptor, Télémaque cries out that he is Télémaque, a man; "free movement set loose on earth, with power to come and go."[32] In a last desperate effort to prove his liberty, he kills himself by hurling himself from a cliff. Mentor advances and cries out above the roar of the sea that suicide is no proof of liberty, that Télémaque died to prove himself free, but that his death proves the opposite. As he finishes pronouncing Télémaque's epitaph—"With Télémaque, chance perished. Now begins the reign of wisdom,"[33] a loosened rock comes hurtling down from above and crushes him while, "on his horses of tenderness, the Lord God burst out laughing like a madman."[34]

V Le Libertinage

This work, published in 1924, contains a series of unusual texts by Aragon including essays, descriptive passages, confessions, a playlet, a short story and pastiches of other writers and styles. The title was intended to shock the bourgeoisie as was its violent, inflammatory preface. "I have never sought anything but scandal and I have sought it for itself," Aragon wrote. He also protested in the preface against the stranglehold upon art exercised by the literary establishment. "Everything that was dictated to me by one passion or another, they transformed into a flash of wit, a manner of speaking. In France, everything ends in flowers of rhetoric."[35] He opposed established artistic traditions and demanded that the artist have complete freedom to realize his potentialities. Nor should the artist be limited by any choice he might make, since no literary adventure is definitive. Aragon added that he wanted each thing that passed through his head to remain there for so short a time that even its faint memory would eventually elude him. In this way, everything that transpired within him would mark a step forward rather than a trace of something that went before. There was nothing that permitted him to judge what his future actions would be, for he did not seek to reconcile his future with his past, nor did he seek to be an excuse for or an example to anyone. As in all of his works from his first to his most recent, Aragon, in this same preface, expressed his faith in love:

I think of nothing except love. My continual distraction in matters of the mind . . . derives from this single, incessant taste for love. For me there is no idea that is not overshadowed by love. Everything that is opposed to love will be destroyed if it is up to me. That is what I am expressing when I claim to be an anarchist.[36]

One of the most interesting texts in this collection, one which anticipates Kafka, is entitled "La Demoiselle aux principes." In this story, a young man experiments on a young woman to evaluate the effects upon her of incomprehensible behavior, of actions without any possible explanation, of words without any possible interpretation. He finds that logical actions, however disturbing they may be, do not cause her anguish, but that he can disconcert her by destroying the logic and order to which she is accustomed. By his continuous actions without motivation, he upsets her equilibrium. Without logic, she can no longer live and kills herself.

In this work, as in *Anicet* and *Le Paysan de Paris*, we find the development of a modern mythology which confers an esthetic value on objects such as shops, streets, automobiles, and newspaper clippings. The décor of the work is no longer woods and waterfalls, but a lady's dressing room with its electric massage machines, nail files, scissors, and curling irons. "The torture chambers of long ago sleep in the hydrotherapy and electric massage equipment."[37] And, as always, there is Aragon's beloved Paris which, "like a garland of flowers crowned my fortunate brow with its cars, its women, and its thousand lights per second."[38]

VI Le Paysan de Paris (The Peasant of Paris)

This work, written in 1926, is the outstanding achievement of Aragon's Surrealist period. The title symbolizes the love of the poet for his city as he compares his emotions to those felt by the peasant for his land. The resonances of this love echo throughout Aragon's work. During the war, when he was exiled from his city, he wrote:

> My poems are made up of that Paris
> My words bear the strange color of her roofs
> The throats of the pigeons glisten and coo there
> I have written more about Paris than about myself
> And suffered more from being without her than
>   from growing old[39]

In the introduction to *Le Paysan de Paris*, "Preface to a Modern Mythology," the young poet described his experiences in quest of surreality. He wrote that one evening, for no apparent reason, everything became bathed in a new, unexpected light. His thoughts no longer followed their normal pattern, but became prey to an overwhelming preoccupation. It was useless to attempt to fight against this distraction. He became what he called "the bottle imp at the command of my senses and of chance. . . . Everything distracts me indefinitely, except from my distraction. A feeling akin to nobility leads me to prefer this abandon to anything else. . . ."[40] Far from fighting against the errors of his senses, he realized that they provided access to a mysterious world that reason could never reveal:

New myths are born along each of our steps. . . . Each day the feeling about life is modified. A mythology waxes and wanes. It is a science which belongs only to those who have had no experience. It is a living science which is self-engendered and destroys itself. Will I still be able, since I am already twenty-six years old, to partake of this miracle? Will I long have the feeling for the wonders of everyday life? I see it diminishing in each man, who advances in his life as if on an increasingly well-paved path, who advances in his familiarity with the world with growing ease, who increasingly throws off his taste for and perception of the unusual. That is what I, desperately, shall never be able to know. [41]

The new myths of which Aragon spoke resulted from a perception of the unusual and the unexpected, from an awareness of the hidden life concealed by every object. Two sections of *Le Paysan de Paris*, "Le Passage de l'Opéra" and "Le Sentiment de la nature aux Buttes-Chaumont," trace his efforts to bring the marvelous of everyday life to light in both the Arcade of the Opéra and the Buttes-Chaumont park.

The Arcade of the Opéra was scheduled to be destroyed to make way for the expansion of the Boulevard Haussmann. Its imminent destruction enhanced its mystical possibilities, and it became the "sanctuary of a cult of the transitory."[42] Even though realistic descriptions are given of the Café de Certâ, which was the meeting place of the Dada group, the restaurants, brothel, bookshop, public baths, theater, cane store, hairdresser, and other tenants of the arcade, everything there appears bathed in a mysterious light. Everything acted upon the receptive mind of the poet to induce hallucinations, hallucinations which he sought to transmit by means of images. It was the image that provided the link between the "still lives set forth by God"[43] and the world of the absolute hidden behind them. "The vice called *Surrealism*," wrote Aragon, "is the passionate use of the stupefying *image* . . . every image at every moment forces you to revise [your concept of] the Universe. And there is for each man, an image that will obliterate the entire Universe."[44]

Using reality as his point of departure, Aragon creates an entirely new world through imagery. While strolling through the Passage de l'Opéra, he pauses at the doorway of the beauty shop for ladies, caught by the idea that men have found only one term of comparison for blond, blond like wheat. But, he asks, have you never seen ferns?

I chewed upon hair like ferns for a whole year. I have known hair of resin, hair of topaz, hair of hysteria. Blond like hysteria, blond like the sky, blond like fatigue, blond like a kiss. On the palette of blondness, I will place the elegance of automobiles, the odor of sainfoin, the silence of mornings, the perplexities of waiting. . . . How blond is the sound of the rain, the song of mirrors. . . . Blond everywhere: I abandon myself to this yellow-pine of the senses, to this concept of blondness that is not the color itself, but a sort of spirit of color wed to accents of love.[45]

The Surrealist fusion of dream and reality is brought about by the imagination. The universe it creates is more real than the visible one. Step right up, calls the imagination,

today I bring you a drug from the limits of the consciousness, from the frontiers of the abyss. What have you sought in drugs up to now if not a feeling of power, a deceitful megalomania and the free exercise of your faculties in the void. . . . You can be sure it is the enemies of order who are circulating this philtre of the absolute. They sneak it past the guards in the form of books, poems. . . . Buy, buy the damnation of your soul, you will destroy yourself at last, here is the machine for capsizing your mind. I announce to the world this page one headline: a new vice has just been born, one madness more has been given to man: *surrealism*, son of frenzy and darkness. Step right up, here is where the kingdoms of the instantaneous begin . . .[46]

In the concluding section of this work, "Le Songe du Paysan," Aragon stated that it was love that was at the basis of the metaphysical state of mind. He described woman as the supreme means of communication with hidden reality. Love represented the confusion of the real and the marvelous, the state of super-reality sought by the Surrealists:

Woman, you take the place of all substance. . . . Charming substitute, you are the sum of a marvelous world, of the natural world, and it is you who reappear when I close my eyes. . . . You are the horizon and the close at hand. . . . The total eclipse. The light. The miracle: and can you think of anything other than the miracle when the miracle is there in its nocturnal garb? Thus the universe little by little dissolves while from its depths rises an adorable phantom.[47]

And, he concluded, poetic activity is the key to love as it is the key to all knowledge: "Be persuaded, you who scoff, that I lead a poetic life."[48]

The observation has been made that *Le Paysan de Paris* mirrors the struggles of the young Surrealists to "juggle chance and destiny, passive automatism and active revolution, optimistic faith in man's future and pessimistic doubt over the disasters of civilization, the conviction that life is here and that life is elsewhere, the marvelous and the absurd."[49]

VII Le Traité du style

Le Traité du style, published in 1928, is an important work in the history of Surrealism. It is not the manual on style it paradoxically announces itself to be in the title, but a violent indictment of the era and an attack on all the intellectual fashions of the period. It strikes at bourgeois writers like Maurois, Mauriac, Gide, and Valéry and at bourgeois great books like *Manon Lescaut*, *Eugénie Grandet*, and *Madame Bovary*. Even Dada is not spared. While Freud, Rimbaud, and Einstein come under fire in this work, it is less against them than against those who have misused and vulgarized their discoveries that Aragon directs his anger. *Le Traité du style* ridicules all the literary themes of the period: departure, escape, adventure, and suicide. All of these, for Aragon, represent a vulgar belief in another world, a far-off paradise. They are no more valid as an escape than the religious solution. None of them offers a satisfactory solution to the problem of existence. Aragon's contention in this work that there is no paradise and that hope is a false attitude of the mind anticipates the works of the existentialists. There is only one way to escape the desperation of life, and that is through humor, which is an enemy of all solutions. By its power to upset reality, humor opens up an infinite number of new poetic possibilities.

The second part of *Le Traité du style* explains and justifies Surrealism and clarifies the theory of automatic writing. Aragon states that Surrealism is not a liberation from literary rules, but a revolt that has taken place outside of literature. Rather than a literary movement, Surrealism is a certain conception of the world built on a revolutionary basis. One must accept the new insights brought by Surrealism, no longer indiscriminately as had previously been the case, but selectively. In a departure from previous theory, Aragon writes here that one must objectively control the results. He takes a second decisive step away from Surrealism when he notes that words cannot be limited to their relationship with the author, but must also take their meaning from the responses they elicit on the part of the reader. Thus, it is in *Le Traité du style* that Aragon moves from the individual toward the collective, from the subjective to the objective.

Aragon's work at this time also gives evidence of new moral considerations. In his last prose work as a Surrealist, *La Peinture au défi*,[50] Aragon wrote that the marvelous came not only from a rejection of reality, but also from the development of the new reality that this rejection had liberated. The end result of the negation of reality is basically ethical in nature, Aragon said, for the marvelous is always the materialization of a moral symbol in violent opposition to the morality of the world surrounding it. Aragon subsequently stated that this attempt to give a new, moral interpretation to the marvelous represented an approach to realism and an attempt to unite his world with the great drama he saw unfolding in the East.

VIII Transitional Works

Aragon has described the texts he wrote from 1925 to 1931 as the history of a progressive disintoxication with words, a transition from Surrealist images to images which echo the cry of the masses and sing the beauty of the revolution. He added that he spent five years caught between the poetic world that he and his friends had forged and the great whirlwind into which he was tempted to throw himself.[51] Aragon's sadness during these years of crisis is reflected in *La Grande Gaieté*, a collection of poems written from 1927 to 1929. Many of them express his despair at the awareness that time was passing rapidly and that he had still not succeeded in building a more beautiful world as he had promised in *Feu de joie*. He cried out that everything was false, including love, on which the Surrealists had founded their greatest expectations. Years later, he revealed that after writing these poems, he attempted suicide during a trip to Venice.

La Grande Gaieté differs from Aragon's earlier works in many ways. The satiric portraits of the bourgeoisie found in this collection, while directly in the line of a great French traditional genre, also prefigure the poems of Communist inspiration. The images here are also different from the Surrealist images which resulted from the rapprochement of two realities with no apparent connection. The greater the distance separating the two terms of the image, the more powerful the image. The goal of the Surrealists was to equal in power the image used by Lautréaumont to describe his Englishman hero: "He is as handsome as . . . the fortuitous encounter on a dissecting table of a sewing machine and an umbrella."[52] In an article written in 1947, Aragon wrote that the Surrealists believed that separating the name from the object it designated was a means of opening a door to a greater reality. For this reason, they used language incorrectly, not as an aid to knowledge, but as an escape; not as a means of expression but as an evocation of what was impossible to express.[53]

In *La Grande Gaieté* and subsequent collections of poetry, the images were used to underline an idea, rather than to dismember it. After his conversion to Communism, Aragon felt that the function of the word was to transcribe reality, not destroy it. And the new image was to bring forth a different message, fraternity instead of individualism, optimistic affirmation of a new world instead of pessimistic despair. Henceforth Aragon would put language at the service of his party and use words for the creation of a new society. As proof of his dedication to the Communist party, Aragon composed the poem "Front Rouge," which was published in *Littérature de la Révolution mondiale*, a journal of the International Writers' Union. This poem was later reprinted in the collection of poems entitled *Persécuté persécuteur* (1931). "Front Rouge" is built on a double antithesis, bourgeois Paris and the struggle of the working man, decadent capitalism and the rise of the Socialist revolution:

> Something nice for my dog
> A drop of champagne Certainly Madame
> We are at Maxim's the year nineteen
> Thirty
> Mats are put under the bottles
> So their aristocratic bottoms
> do not come in contact with life's difficulties[54]

He balances this satire with descriptions of the demonstrations of the working men that have struck fear into the hearts of the bourgeoisie. He calls upon the workers to kill the police, and then,

> On, on towards the west where sleep
> rich children and first-class tarts
> past the Madeleine Proletariat
> Some day you'll blow up the Arc de Triomphe
> Proletariat learn your strength
> Learn your strength and release it[55]

Together with social satire and revolutionary fervor, we find in *Persécuté persécuteur* the poem "I do not know how to Play Golf," Aragon's first love poem to Elsa:

> I have seen the map of this city
> and it is your shadow my love
> exactly your shadow when the sun
> places on the nape of your neck this knot of
>   fiery ribbons
> that is ravishingly becoming to you [56]

Aragon also uses here for the first time a theme that will recur throughout his work. It stresses the intimate link joining the individual to the rest of society, bringing with it the impossibility of individual happiness in the midst of universal distress: "I love and none the less life is intolerable. . ./I love and we love each other but in the midst of a shipwreck."[57]

Hourra l'Oural, an epic poem describing the rise of socialism in Russia, is dedicated to anti-Fascist militants who were killed during the attempted Fascist putsch in France in February, 1934. The poet wished to pay hommage to them as he sang of the Urals and of the new Communist man. This is the first of Aragon's works in which the subject is completely external. The revolution depicted here is the positive world of the future being constructed in the Soviet Union rather than the destructive rebellion of *Persécuté persécuteur*: "It is the country of Leninism with hand on shovel/That answers the call of the future five years ahead of time."[58] During the 1920s, Aragon had attacked those forces of society that would prevent man from living freely according to his desires. In *Hourra l'Oural*, he attacks these same forces, but now as oppressors of the working people rather than of the artist. He decrees death for all those who would endanger the October Revolution. Previously, his anger had been directed against entire groups or against stereotyped members of these groups. In this collection, stereotypes are often replaced by distinct personalities, names are mentioned and individual portraits are painted: "They looked well when they were getting off the train/Nicolas II held by the hand his little Scotch/plaid sausage of the empire."[59]

In keeping with the Communist ideology, there is no trace of nationalistic sentiment in either *Hourra l'Oural* or *Persécuté persécuteur*. In both, Aragon advocates an international entente of the working people of the world:

> I salute here
> The International above the Marseillaise
> Give way oh Marseillaise
> to the International for here is
> the autumn of your days here is
> the October in which your last strains are obliterated [60]

He expressed antipathy for France which, together with the other capitalist countries, was attempting to subvert the Communist cause.

Throughout *Hourra l'Oural*, Aragon sought to demonstrate that poetry was not an end in itself, as he had formerly believed, but the expression of contemporary reality. Despite certain lyrical passages in the work, it is more a political tract than poetry. It was not until the German invasion of France that Aragon was to reveal himself as a great French lyric poet.

CHAPTER 3

Poet of the French Resistance

After 1939, in the face of the German menace, a new nationalistic sentiment entered into the poetry of Louis Aragon. Poetry was no longer to represent the search for an absolute, nor the invention of a super language, nor a weapon to be used against the bourgeoisie, but an attempt to define transcendent values and to give a meaning to the French struggle against the Fascist invaders. In a letter written in 1941, Aragon described the change that had taken place in his poetic aims: "First we worked over the problem of language so carefully that nothing seemed worthy of it; nothing seemed worthwhile saying. We said nothing magnificently and with the greatest freedom of expression. And now we have found what we had to say, more than we had ever dreamed. Can we ever say it well enough? "[1]

Le Crève-coeur (*Heartbreak*), the first of Aragon's wartime collections of poetry, was begun just before the war, interrupted in May, 1940 and completed during the days of the defeat and the three months following it. This book, which was published in London, Canada, and Algeria, was the first sign received in the outside world that the spirit of France was still alive: "But suddenly Louis Aragon of France cried out far off as by deep walls imprisoned. Liberty, he said ..."[2] Aragon later said that without these verses, without this confidence in the message he had to transmit, without his refusal to abandon his belief in human dignity, he would not have been able to survive the defeat and the occupation.[3]

The verses of *Le Crève-coeur* are a chronicle of France under the stress of war and the Nazi occupation. The two world wars, separated by only twenty years, seem to merge into a continuous nightmare as the poet watches the young boys, for whom his generation had fought, called to war in their turn:

> Twenty years Scarcely time enough for a
> childhood and is it not
> An atrocious penitence for our middle years
> To see again after twenty years the little babies
> Of that time march out with us again[4]

He is filled with regret for his beloved whom he has left behind and compares his loneliness and boredom with the sentiments of the other soldiers, in the poems, "I Await her Letter at Sunset" and "The Time of Crossword Puzzles." With great bitterness, the poet describes the twenty-year-olds as, "Good for the wind, good for the night, good for the cold/Good for marching and for mud and for bullets."[5] The beauty of the summer described in "The Lilacs and the Roses" makes even more unbearable the French defeat. There is ironic contradiction throughout the poem between the vivid colors of the flowers and the darkness of panic, the fragrance of violets and the stench of death:

> O months of blooming months of transformations
> May without a cloud and June cut to the heart
> I shall never forget either the lilacs or the roses
> Or those whom spring kept folded away
> . . . .
> I shall never forget the gardens of France
> Like illuminations of past centuries
> Or the trouble of dusk the mystery of the silence
> The roses all along the road we traveled
> The lie given by the flowers to the wind of panic
> To the soldiers who passed by on the wings of fear
> . . . .
> They told us that night that Paris had surrendered
> I shall never forget the lilacs and the roses
> Nor shall I forget the two loves we lost[6]

These poems also depict the horror of the German invasion, the mining villages of the Pas de Calais emptied of their inhabitants, and the exodus. From Shakespeare's *King Richard II*,[7] Aragon takes the leitmotif of his poem "Richard II Quarante," "I remain king of my sorrows":

> My country is a river boat
> Abandoned by the haulers
> And I am like that unfortunate king
> More unfortunate than misfortune
> Who yet remained king of his sufferings [8]

The joy of being reunited with his wife after the surrender is destroyed by his knowledge of the misfortune of his country:

> My love I was in your arms
> Outside someone hummed
> An old French song
> I understood at last my suffering
> And its refrain like a bare foot
> Rippled the green water of silence[9]

This theme of the impossibility of individual happiness in the midst of universal despair recurs throughout Aragon's work.

Recognizing at this time the unique value of rhyme as an aid to the retention and transmission of songs, Aragon sought to rehabilitate rhyme and restore it to its former position of importance in French poetry. In consequence, he rhymed all of the verses in *Le Crève-coeur*. This rhyme cannot be reproduced in translation without altering the meaning of the poems, a practice that has been condemned by Aragon, who places content above form: "My verses have been translated into Russian and into other languages. My translators, even those who were good poets, made me long to be translated into prose. Because, for me, the meaning of what I write (in verse as well as in prose) is what I am least prepared to sacrifice in the voyage from one language to another . . ."[10]

In "La Rime en 1940," Aragon attributed the decline of French rhyme to the fact that modern poets believed that all rhymes had already been used or that no new rhymes could be invented. "I say that it is not true that there are no new rhymes in this new world," wrote Aragon. "Almost everything we come up against in this strange war, which is the landscape of an unknown and terrible poetry, is new to the language and still alien to poetry. . . . Thus rhyme regains its dignity because it serves to introduce new things into the old, elevated language, which is its own goal, and which is called poetry. Then rhyme ceases to be a mockery, because it . . . is the link of the chain that joins things to song, and that makes things sing."[11]

There were some poets and technicians at the beginning of the twentieth century who were aware of the necessity of restoring rhyme to its former distinction. Aragon mentioned, in particular, the contribution made by the poet Guillaume Apollinaire, whose redefinition of masculine and feminine rhymes was adopted by Aragon. For the Classical and Romantic French poets, the presence or absence of a mute *e* at the end of a word was the basis for defining masculine and feminine rhymes. Apollinaire, on the other hand, was concerned with the sounds of his rhymes rather than with the spelling. He classified as feminine all words ending in a pronounced consonant (whether followed or not by a mute *e*), and as masculine all words ending in either an oral or nasal vowel or in a vowel followed by an unpronounced consonant or an unpronounced mute *e*. Thus, as is the case in spoken French, in one of Aragon's poems "ciel" rhymes with "elle" and "querelles" in defiance of traditional rules of versification.

To the redefinition of masculine and feminine rhymes, Aragon added the modern enjambement in which not only the meaning, but also the sound, runs over into the next line; the rhyme straddles the end of one line and the beginning of the next. This type of rhyme infinitely increases the number of possible rhyme schemes, as does the "rime complex," in which several words or parts of words compose the rhyming element.

II Les Yeux d'Elsa *and* "Arma virumque cano"

Les Yeux d'Elsa appeared two years after the publication of *Le Crève-coeur*. It contained poems written from December, 1940 to February, 1942 in the unoccupied zone of France. During this period, Aragon suffered greatly for his country, for it seemed as if his beloved France would never be free, as if the nightmare of the German occupation would never end. In four of the poems in this collection, the poet made frequent use of the image of darkness and night to symbolize his despair:[12] "Night of May," "Night of Dunkirk," "Night in Broad Daylight," and "Night of Exile." In the "Night of Exile," the banished poet recalls his beloved Paris:

> Do you remember those nights It hurts me to
>   remember them
> They had as many flashes of light as the
>   black eyes of doves
> Nothing of those jewels of darkness is left
>   to us
> Now we know what night really is
> . . . .
> Will we ever see again the far off paradise
> The Halles the Opéra the Concorde and the Louvre
> Those nights do you remember them when the night
>   covers us
> The night that comes from the heart and that has
>   no dawn[13]

The poem "More Beautiful Than Tears" was provoked by Drieu la Rochelle, Aragon's former friend who had become a Nazi collaborator and who had denounced Aragon's clandestine activity. He accused him of being the leader and organizer of Resistance writers in France and the author of clandestine attacks against the Germans and the Vichy government. To this denunciation, Aragon replied with his poem which was read over the Algiers radio by General de Gaulle:

> I prevent some people from breathing freely
>   while I am alive
> I trouble their sleep with untold remorse
> It seems that my poems unlock the brasses
> And that they make a noise to awaken the dead[14]

No oppressor could condemn him to silence or prevent him from loving France. Even hope of personal survival did not matter, if only France might live again:

> What does it matter if I die before
> The sacred visage is reborn
> Let us dance oh my child let us dance in a ring
> My country is hunger misery and love[15]

The war must end, wrote Aragon, and mankind must emerge triumphant:

> My love has but one name it is youthful hope
> I always hear again its new symphony
> And you who hear it in the depths of suffering
> Raise your eyes beautiful sons of France
> My love has but one name My hymn has ended[16]

In the poems of *Les Yeux d'Elsa*, Aragon's wife assumed an even greater role than before, a role that was to grow with each succeeding work: "Even if all those who would in a single blasphemy deny both love and what I love, were powerful enough to crush the last spark of this fire of France, I hold up before them this small paper book, this misery of words, this lost gibberish; and what does it matter what happens to it if, in the hour of the greatest hatred, I have for one instant shown to this country that has been torn apart, the resplendent face of love."[17]

The rehabilitation of French poetry, begun in "La Rime en 1940," is continued by Aragon in the preface to *Les Yeux d'Elsa*, the title of which is taken from Virgil: "Arma virumque cano" ("I Sing of Arms and the Man"). Here Aragon affirmed that his attempt to give meaning and life to the art of versification in the previous essay had been only a first step. He continued his defense of French rhyme, which he described as the element that had liberated French poetry from Latin domination and had created a truly national poetry. It was also by means of rhyme that he hoped to secure wide popularity for his poems and to re-establish the contact that had existed between the poet and the people during the Middle Ages.

"La Leçon de Ribérac," an article written in 1941 to illustrate the continuity of French tradition, was appended to the 1945 edition of *Les Yeux d'Elsa*. In Ribérac, a small town on the Dordogne River to which Aragon and Elsa went in their first distress after the armistice, had lived the poet Arnaud Daniel, recognized as a master by both Dante and Petrarch. What fascinated Aragon about this man was not only the incredible invention of new rules and disciplines that he had imposed upon himself and then varied from poem to poem, but also the fact that he had developed this poetry in one of the most troubled periods of French history. From Arnaud Daniel, Aragon proceeded to a discussion of the golden age of French medieval literature, the second half of the twelfth century. It was then that the French language came into its own, and poetic genres with their accompanying refinements were created. At this time, too, the great poetic themes, including love of country, were born. During the twelfth century, French poetry influenced all of Europe and carried with it the *morale courtoise*, a code of ethics which taught justice, chivalry, defense of the weak, and high ideals. Aragon concluded this article, expressing the hope that contemporary poets, strengthened by French history and tradition, would emulate their predecessors and create a new dawn of French culture and influence.

III Le Musée Grévin

This long poem of satire and invective appeared in the summer of 1943, "the fourth summer of our apocalypse,"[18] when occupied France, "a country devastated by the plague,"[19] was awaiting the opening of a sencond front. Aragon signed this poem with the pseudonym François la Colère, or François the Wrathful. Patterned on *Les Châtiments* of Victor Hugo, which were directed against the dictatorship of Louis Napoléon, Aragon turned his wrath against the Nazis and their Vichy supporters. He predicted their imminent defeat: "They carry in their flesh the terrible stigmata/Of what is going to happen and which they disguise in vain."[20] He wrote to give resonance to his hatred and told of the hell of Auschwitz, which had already swallowed up one hundred French women:

> I salute you Maries of France with a hundred
>   different faces
> . . . .
> When you return for you must return
> There will be as many flowers as you desire
> There will be flowers the color of the future
> There will be flowers when you return[21]

The poem terminated on a note of hope with a long hymn of praise to France, delivered of phantoms and returned to peace:

> I salute you my France with eyes of turtledove
> Never too great my torment never too much my love
> My France my new and my eternal theme
> Soil strewn with heroes sky full of sparrows[22]

IV   Brocéliande, En Français dans le texte *and*
     "De l'exactitude historique en poésie"

While all of Aragon's poetic treatises during this period counseled a return to national poetry and regular verse, he added, in "De l'exactitude historique en poésie," that he had never thought of turning these elements into a religion in the fashion of many schools of poetry. Regular verse was merely an aid to transmission of his message at this time. He further explained that he used French history and legends in his poetry in order to camouflage the meaning of his words from the Germans. He could not attack them directly but could refer to them indirectly by evoking former miseries of France. It was not difficult for his French readers to grasp his exact meaning. His over-all plan was to contrast the grandeur of France to the Nazi racial myths. Although characters like Tristan and Lancelot and settings like the forest of Brocéliande[23] came from legend, they were still part of the French heritage and reminded the French people of the former glories of their country. Aragon wanted these myths to lead not only to reflection, but to action. To those who might reproach him for having borrowed from the old Celtic traditions instead of realistically photograph-ing the horrors of German tyranny in France, Aragon replied that it was not only the censor who made this necessary, but also his belief that, by ignoring the transitory reality of the defeat and shame of France, he was affirming the eternal reality and glory of France.[24]

France in 1942, wrote Aragon, resembled Brocéliande. In the forest, the Vichy "sorcerers" and the German "dragons" had perverted the meaning of words. As time went on and the tyranny increased, there were more and more knights-errant in the Resistance movement. Thus history gave an added reality to the legend reincarnated in his poem. Despite its seeming difficulty and learned references, *Brocéliande* became extremely popular, a sort of breviary of the new chivalry. The young Catholic hero Gilbert Dru had the book in his pocket when he was arrested. Aragon's former anti-Catholic sentiments had been forgotten in the common struggle. He had learned to respect the faith of his companions in the Resistance. Although he could not share their views, he had reached a new state of maturity where he could perceive "what is generous and human in this divine faith. In a word, what is French. [A belief that] before the enemy of my nation sang in harmony with my disbelief, a concept of man that the Communist and the Christian may have, but never the Nazi."[25]

One of Aragon's most famous wartime poems, "The Rose and the Reed," dedicated to both Catholics and Communists alike, described their common heroic exploits:

He who believed in God
He who did not believe
Both adored the beauty
Prisoner of the soldiers
Which one mounted the ladder
And which one watched out below
He who believed in God
He who did not believe

. . . .
Both were faithful
With their lips hearts and arms
And both said that she would live again
And that he who lived would see it
He who believed in God
He who did not believe

. . . .
Sing flute or cello of
The double love which burned
The lark and the swallow
The rose and the reed[26]

"He who believed in God" and "He who did not believe" reappear in one of the stories of the collection *Servitude et Grandeur des Français*, subtitled *Scènes des années terribles*. The seven stories in this collection, each depicting a facet of the occupation, were all written before the liberation and show the heroic and grotesque sides of French life under Nazi domination. Both Aragon's prose and poetic works of this period reflect his determination to be a spokesman for those who fought against or fell to the Nazis. His "Art Poétique," which appeared in the collection *En Français dans le texte*, expresses his resolve to write henceforth only for his "friends who died in May."[27]

V La Diane française (French Reveille)

La Diane française juxtaposes the France of legend and romance and the new France of sabotage and the Resistance; it tells of the part played by song and poetry in keeping alive the spirit of revolt. Here Aragon wrote that the French had taken their country for granted and that the only thing that characterized it was its language, a beautiful language that had been used indiscriminately. The French knew that France was a country only because of the passports they carried in their pockets. But, like Vercingétorix, the great leader of the Gauls who was killed by Caesar after surrendering, they learned the price of surrender. And then, continued Aragon, we sang softly in our fashion. The refrains we hummed spread. You know, when you pass someone on the sidewalks of a large city and take up from him the catchy tune he was whistling, and transmit it without realizing it to another man you pass, who goes further on and carries it with him. Our song swelled, was taken up again and again and multiplied. What infinite echoes does a people conceal, what mysteries! . . . My country became a deep, dull rumbling like the sea when it approaches the cliffs, like the boat vibrating at the port. My country became the very song of the world, the music which finally summed up all the hope and all the despair. . . . My country approached the light as it sang! . . . Then French reveille sounded.[28]

The story of the death of the Communist Resistance hero Gabriel Péri had been passed along orally and, based on the facts he received, Aragon wrote a poem for the second anniversary of Péri's death, entitled "La Légende de Gabriel Péri":

> It is in the cemetery at Ivry
> That in the depths of the common grave
> In the anonymous moonless night
> Rests Gabriel Péri
> Yet the martyr in his tomb
> Still disturbs his assassins
> Miracles are possible in holy places
> Where the tears of the people fall
> . . . .
> Dread exemplary deaths
> Tyrants who massacre in vain
> They are a terrible wine
> For a people and its anger[29]

In a note appended to this poem, Aragon explained that the subject matter it contained stemmed from legend and not from history. It was not at Ivry, but at Suresnes, not in a common ditch, but in a registered grave, that Gabriel Péri was buried. The poet did not invent any of the details used in his poem, but had received this distorted version orally. Thus a modern legend was born about the exploits of a famous hero, just as had occurred in the days of the *Chansons de geste* when the troubadours carried their tales throughout France.

Typical of Resistance poems, written to be circulated clandestinely and to be learned by heart, were those in which a man refused to save himself by betraying his comrades. Aragon deals with this theme in the "Ballad of One who Sang at the Stake." The refrain "And if I had to do it over, I would follow this road again,"[30] was a phrase that recurred in farewell letters written by many Resistance heroes.

And if I had to do it over
I would follow this road again
A voice rose from the iron chains
And spoke of the future

They say that in his cell
Two men on that night
Whispered to him Give in
Are you tired of this life

You can live you can live
You can live like us
Say the word that will free you
And you can live on your knees
. . . .
I die and France lives
My love and my refusal
Oh my friends if I die
You know the reason why[31]

Other poems from *La Diane française* like "Christmas Roses" and "Elsa at the Mirror" achieved a popularity unknown for poetry in modern times. In this collection, Aragon fully realized his ambition:

To find words as strong as madness
To find words the color of each day
To find words that no one will forget
Lights for the blind and thunder for the deaf[32]

In 1944, when France had been liberated, Aragon decided to reconcile and unite the patriotic poet and the revolutionary. We see the beginning of this trend in "From the Poet to his Party," the concluding poem of *La Diane française*, where he attributed his Resistance activities and his patriotism to his Communist teachings:

My party gave me back my eyes and my memory
I no longer knew even what a child knows
That my blood was so red and my heart was French
I only knew that the night was black
My party gave me back my eyes and my memory[33]

VI Le Nouveau Crève-coeur *and* Chroniques du
bel canto

When the war ended, Aragon did not abandon political poetry. He ridiculed those who urged him to return to the theme of "eternal man."

He maintained that German imperialism had been replaced by the social domination of the bourgeoisie and, as *Le Crève-coeur* of 1940 was inspired by the German occupation of 1940, so *Le Nouveau Crève-coeur*, the new heartbreak, stemmed from the post-liberation abuses of the traditional enemy, the bourgeoisie. The defeat of this enemy was as essential for the welfare of the French people as was the defeat of the Germans, and Aragon once again sounded the call to action, lest the French find themselves subjugated by the former French "valets" of the Germans. Solidarity with all factions of French life gave way to partisanship, Communist against non-Communist, worker against bourgeois. Thus, the cycle started in 1930 runs its course, although in *Le Nouveau Crève-coeur* Aragon couches his demands in the more guarded language of the Communists of the postwar period. His demands for the rights of the working man are no longer inflammatory calls to assassination, but are pleas for progress and justice made in the name of France and not of the international Communist movement.

Pure poetry, when reflecting eternals, is enduring, but Aragon was not concerned with the future life of his poems. He was writing for those about him and, when conditions changed, so did his poems. In *Chroniques du bel canto*, Aragon's first postwar work on poetic technique, he explained that even though the battle against the Germans was over, each new day brought new battles which required a new, modern poetry. In this work, Aragon spoke of "le chant"—"the song," which is what distinguishes poetry from prose.

There are places in which everything is music, abandon, fluttering of wings, a beach for the bare feet of memory. There are places which fill the heart to overflowing as does a melody, which have the warm plenitude of tears, that light before nightfall in the summer of childhood, that banal mystery of a bird which suddenly lets you draw near, I do not know what quality of a daydream inexplicably linked for me to scattered violets. There are places where the silence itself sings. . . . There are verses that are the sum of these deserts, this shadow, this evening, these perfumes from nowhere. There are verses as deep as potions, as heavy as clouds, there are verses as light as tears, as troubling as mirrors.[34]

The principal enemy of song is ignorance, continued Aragon. He maintained that poetry should be explained, for, when the mystery of the poem is removed, it assumes its legitimate role which is to enlighten, not to confuse. For this reason, he sought to discredit the spontaneous, primitive, and artless poetry which seeks to deny that there is a science of poetry. When perfect harmony exists between content and form, when that so-called subjectivity of the poet touches something within the reader who understands him then, according to Aragon, the verses sing: "There is music only when the sound emitted awakens harmonies in that crystal at the other end of the room, which *understands* so well, and feels that this sound is so truly *musical*, that it breaks because of it. That is why I demand of poetry, whether clear or not, notes, historical details, which far from preventing me from dreaming, give to my dream the immense field of reality."[35]

CHAPTER 4

The Real World

I Les Cloches de Bâle (The Bells of Basel)

Louis Aragon wrote in *J'Abats mon jeu* that novels saved him from the honorable destiny of medicine that had been chosen for him: "I had read too many novels to limit myself to illnesses of the human body, and soon I began to write them, because I had to give that form to my dreams which had been nourished by the sort of imagination that remains forever young and alive in books . . . where each person, even the most miserable of men and women, can find love, beauty, music, and everything that makes the greatness of dreams and the humanity of man."[1] Aragon has said that he learned to write novels while writing *Les Cloches de Bâle* (1934), the novel that was to become the first in the series "Le Monde réel" ("The Real World"). The novels which comprise this series, except for an epilogue added to the fourth novel, *Aurélien*, take place in the period from 1880 through the 1920s. The object of these novels is to present a history of this period, characterized principally by the struggle of the bourgeoisie to maintain its money and privileges and to prevent the rise of the working class.

Les Cloches de Bâle centers on the destinies of three women, the fictional Diane de Nettencourt and Catherine Simonidzé, and the real Clara Zetkin, one of the founders of the German Communist party. According to Aragon, it is in *Les Cloches de Bâle* that he first attempted to adapt modern reality to his ideology. He shows in this novel the conflicting class interests in France and the preparation for war.

Diane de Nettencourt, the protagonist of the first section of the novel, is a beautiful courtesan who lives only for money and luxury. She is the symbol of a society founded on financial values, in which women are a commodity for sale. It is a society of "men who pretend to be worthy of their way of life, of women who tremble all their lives for fear of losing these men and, with them, two or three domestics, an apartment and dresses."[2] Love is impossible in a milieu where woman has no existence except in respect to the money men give her. Diane, while engaged in liaisons with many men, including the magnate Wisner, who will appear throughout the novels of "Le Monde réel," marries the enormously wealthy Georges Brunel. When a young career officer from a noble family kills himself in Brunel's home, it is revealed that Brunel is a usurer. He is divorced by Diane, who has succeeded in transferring their assets to her own name, and is ostracized by society. Brunel unmasks the hypocrisy of this society when he states that if he made his money buying shares in the casino at Monte Carlo, which is responsible for hundreds of suicides each year, or in the de Beers mines, where they think nothing of slitting open the bellies of the Black miners to find missing diamonds, or in the opium traffic, or in any colonial exploitation supported by the government, he would be given the Legion of Honor instead of being condemned to disgrace. If he no longer lends to a Pierre de Sabran to keep a courtesan, but to the Turks to massacre the Greeks or to the English to exploit the Hindu, then he is no longer a usurer, he is a stockholder who clips coupons, surrounded by admiration and deference.[3]

Brunel visits Wisner to determine whether he can still count on his aid although he has committed the unforgivable crime of being caught. We then discover that Brunel has been a front for Wisner, who has supplied the funds for his usurious loans. When Wisner demands repayment of one hundred thousand francs that Brunel still owes him, Brunel refuses and tells him that he leaves him his wife in exchange. The cynical Wisner replies that, as Brunel knows, Diane has been his mistress for years and that she is no longer Brunel's to give. Brunel asks Wisner to set him up elsewhere, but he refuses because he has found a better outlet for his speculations, Morocco. Wisner then explains: "All the same, it is a bit more exciting to lend money for an enterprise of this nature than to play your little game of 100% interest with characters like that Sabran, who stupidly compromises the whole game by blowing out his brains. In my game, Sabrans by the hundreds are pawns in a much more interesting match, and if they are killed en route, well, at least it is for something! Dead on the field of honor is more glorious than suicide! A beautiful good colony still remains, [with] mines, agricultural products, cities, ports, roads, railroads."[4] To rid himself of Brunel who might embarrass him, Wisner proposes to send him to Morocco. When Brunel refuses to leave France, Wisner obtains a position for him in the police department. It is in this function that he reappears at the end of the novel as one of the men planning to assassinate the great French Socialist leader Juarès.

When Aragon showed the first section of *Les Cloches de Bâle* to Elsa, she asked him why he was writing it and to whom it would prove useful. It was her question that changed the direction of the novel, the second part of which centers around Catherine Simonidzé, a young Georgian who was patterned after a guest at the pension run by Aragon's family. Catherine marks the transition between the woman of the past, represented by Diane, and the enlightened free woman of the future, Clara Zetkin.

Les Cloches de Bâle demonstrates the ultimate impossibility of love between people with differing concepts of the world. Catherine and a young career officer, Jean Thiébault, spend an idyllic vacation together in the mountains of Savoy. This brief period of love and peace contrasts prominently with the remainder of their lives. Their vacation is interrupted when they see a crowd of workers marching through the village of Cluses toward the watch factory. Suddenly, shots rings out from a house and several men are killed. In their rage, the workers decide to burn the house. Jean cries out: "They want to burn the house. Stop them! " But Catherine grasps his wrist. Looking into her eyes, he sees that he has lost her. "They want to burn the house," he repeats. "They are right," replies Catherine and releases his wrist.[5]

The following day, Catherine learns that the factory has burned down, but that the house was untouched. The assassins are in prison. Without factory and without proprietors, the strike has ended. Now it is the turn of another manufacturer to take over the workers and the clientele of the defunct factory. The strike has served only to further monopolize the industry. And Jean cannot understand that it is abominable that the strike, with its struggle, misery, and death, should lead only to a concentration that will profit one individual. By his inability to comprehend the basic injustice of this situation, Jean becomes further and further removed from Catherine. He belongs to another world; he is an enemy.

After breaking with Jean, Catherine tries to find a meaning for her life. She discovers the anarchist group in Paris through their newspaper. The anti-militarism of the anarchists reflects the attitude of Catherine, which is mainly the product of her revolt against all men and their domination of women. One day, she sees the crippled anarchist leader beaten to death by the police as he attempts to defend himself with his crutches. Each day, her alienation from the rest of society becomes more evident to her. She has broken with her class, but she is unable to take the step to ally herself with the workers, for whom she feels profound sympathy. She is torn between two worlds; her humanism links her to the exploited while the check she receives each month from her father's oil wells in Bakù binds her to the bourgeoisie. In desperation, she attempts to commit suicide, but is prevented from throwing herself into the Seine by a young worker, a taxi driver. Catherine helps the workers during a strike of the taxi drivers in 1912, but she is not really a part of their movement. Her livelihood is not in question, nor does she belong to their class. She is, in reality, helping the strikers in order to solve her own personal problems. Victor, the personification of the good, Communist worker,—a type that figured in so many Soviet books and movies of the twenties and thirties,—remains a lifeless symbol. Perhaps the reason for his inability to infuse life into the workers was given by Aragon when he wrote that, basically, he is not a novelist. With him it is a question of ideas to which he attempts to give a face and a body.[6]

Catherine has taken the first step away from the world of the bourgeoisie towards the world of the future in which woman will be the equal of man. She has left behind the society in which women are parasites and approaches the world of work. But, writes Aragon, "I can no longer speak of Catherine. Hesitating, vacillating Catherine, how slowly does she approach the light! "[7] The light toward which Catherine is groping shines in the eyes of Clara Zetkin, the woman of the future, who has taken her rightful place alongside of man. She was the *raison d'être* of the novel. With her, the social problem of woman was finally solved. When she appeared at the International Congress against War, which was held in Bâle in 1912, Clara Zetkin was over fifty years old. "She is not beautiful, but there is something strong in her, which transcends woman. . . . You cannot help but notice her in a crowd. She is dressed rather carelessly, but it is not her streaked dresses nor the fur piece awkwardly perched on her shoulders which catch the eye, which draw attention to her. What is unusual in her are her eyes." Aragon then interrupts the narrative to describe his feelings when he saw Clara Zetkin twenty years later in Moscow when she was worn out by age and sickness. Even then, she had those "magnificent, enormous eyes, the eyes of all working class Germany, blue and mobile, like deep waters cut through with currents. They partook of phosphorescent seas and of the legendary ancestor, the old German Rhine."[8]

For Clara, social problems are no different from those besetting men. Here, concludes the modern troubadour, ends the old *chanson de geste* and begins the new romance. "Here for the first time in the world, a place is given to true love. One that is not soiled by the hierarchy of man over woman, by the sordid story of dresses and kisses, by the financial domination by man of woman. . . . The woman of modern times has been born, and it is of her that I sing. And it is of her that I will sing."[9]

II *Theoretical Works on Socialist Realism*

In a series of theoretical works written in the early 1950s, Aragon explained that all of his novels were constructed according to the doctrine of Socialist Realism. This doctrine was defined at the first All-Union Congress of Soviet Writers in Moscow, in 1934, as the basic method of Soviet belles-lettres and literary criticism. It demanded of the artist a "truthful, historically concrete representation of reality in its revolutionary development."[10] Aragon expounded upon and developed this theory in many works devoted to the application of Socialist Realism in poetry, prose, and art. He saluted Courbet, Stendhal, and Victor Hugo as significant ancestors of Socialist Realism in France: Courbet because he was the first to proclaim in painting the primacy of matter, the independent existence of the object in relationship to the artist, the absolute necessity to paint according to nature and to paint solely according to nature what the eye saw, and only what it saw. It was Courbet who broke with idealism, his painting affirmed with all his materialistic faith, the belief in the existence of the external world.[11]

True realism, wrote Aragon in another technical work, *La Lumière de Stendhal* (*The Light of Stendhal*),[12] has its roots in national traditions, in the great writers of a country's past, like Stendhal in France. Stendhal's *Le Rouge et le noir* was a work that prepared the revolution of July, 1830. At the height of the Romantic period, Stendhal emerged as a "critical realist," one who mirrored his time selectively. Selective realism can become scientific realism in which the novel is based on the social, political, and economic relationships of the characters and in which the movement follows the movement of history. By explaining and criticizing reality, Stendhal contributed to the transformation of this reality, not in the direction of socialism, but toward liberal democracy, a great step forward at that time and an important one in the history of Socialist Realism. The raison d'être of his work was the education and transformation of men in the spirit of the future.[13]

Not only does French Socialist Realism have its roots in the immense inheritance of the past, writes Aragon, but it also keeps it alive and explains it. Socialist Realism, which implies a critical re-evaluation of the national heritage, must assure the continuity of a national literature. It is not placed outside of history, but is part of a given society at a given period. Based upon the experiences of the past, Socialist Realism takes its methods from the Naturalists with their insistence upon detail. However, it is not content to merely transcribe these details; it interprets facts and details, gives them meaning and force and integrates them into the movement of humanity. Thus, Socialist Realism is distinguishable from Naturalism with its supposed objectivity, because it portrays only what it chooses to reproduce.[14]

III Les Beaux Quartiers (*1936*)

This novel, which was translated into English as *Residential Quarter*, is the second volume in the series "Le Monde réel." In the postface to the novel, Aragon wrote that he had named the series in memory of the long struggle that had gone on within him before he left the world of shadows to enter the real world. "As I did with *Les Cloches de Bâle*," he continued, "I dedicate both what I have written here and what I will write, I dedicate the 'Real World' to Elsa Triolet, to whom I owe everything that I am, to whom I owe having found, in the depths of my confusion, the entrance to the real world where living and dying are worthwhile."[15]

Two brothers, Armand and Edmond Barbentane, dominate this vast panorama of French life which, like *Les Cloches de Bâle*, covers the period from the closing years of the nineteenth century to the eve of World War I. In the manner of the traditional novel, it tells a story, portrays characters, describes real events, and mixes autobiography and history with the story. The author does not intervene directly but seeks to convince by a dispassionate presentation of facts. The novel is divided like a nineteenth-century novel between Paris and the provinces and traces the passage of the protagonists from the village of their childhood to the city, in search of their destiny. The first part of the novel takes place in the fictional town of Sérianne-le-Vieux, principal town of its district in Savoy, ruled by a "potbellied sovereign," the owner of the chocolate factory. "There is nothing but the most expected, the most down to earth in this village where kings no longer stop," and over which floats a sweet, penetrating odor of chocolate, "like gangrene on the fields of battle."[16]

Aragon presents a realistic portrayal of the town, its aristocracy, bourgeoisie, petite bourgeoisie and, to a lesser extent, the French workers and, at the bottom of the ladder, the Italian workers who work for half pay and live in deplorable misery. This novel, like the others in the series, is characterized by its concentration on the upper and middle classes. Even the social rebels come from the bourgeoisie. Aragon justified this by stating that there was so much more to write about the ruling class, because they have so much more time in which to live, while the workers have time only to work. "That is perhaps what separates most vividly the bourgeoisie from the proletariat. The bourgeois speak at length about those among them who work. But work that provides more than mere sustenance, work that does not leave one with only enough time to recuperate strength for the next day's work; the work of those who possess, of those who amass wealth, cannot be compared to the work of the workingman, except by an abominable play on words."[17]

Armand Barbentane, the younger son of Doctor Barbentane, mayor of Sérianne, is destined for the priesthood by his frustrated, bitter mother, principally because of her desire to avenge herself on her free-thinking husband. Armand gives himself wholeheartedly to religion. His confessor urges him to join a pro Fascist group, *Pro Patria*, organized by Adrien Arnaud, the son of the local department store owner. Arnaud has observed that during strikes it is difficult to find scabs who know how to work the machines. His plan is to assemble a large squad of young men from bourgeois families and to teach them the fundamentals of each industry so that they will be able to fill in to break any threatened strike. They will be trained to work in factories, on streetcars, and in gas and electric companies, so that there will always be personnel ready in case of strikes. This training can be linked to military training, because the young volunteers will have to learn to defend themselves against the workers, by force of arms, if necessary.

Armand becomes apprenticed to a streetcar conductor, but he soon realizes that what he is doing is wrong. His Catholic studies have left him with a vague idea of social injustice, and he is uncomfortable in the role he is now playing. He expresses to his confessor his growing doubts. His confessor's evasive answers disturb Armand, who begins to find poetry superior to religion: "It is the cult of Beauty, it explains what Abbé Petitjeanin refuses to consider; it justifies bursts of enthusiasm for great Ideas, women; it is mixed with this terrible and magnificent feeling, Love, whose very name the Holy Books themselves had to borrow to win mens' hearts."[18]

The death of a worker in a fight with the *Pro Patria* group and the suicide of a maid, tormented by her employer and abandoned by Armand's friend, further undermine all that he has previously accepted: "What was the . . . meaning of all those dreadful things? He could not say. He did not have the plan. From all that emerged only the feeling of a monstrous injustice, of a triumphant injustice . . . at whose mercy one found oneself in proportion to his poverty or his sensitivity."[19] Unable to find the answers to these questions in Sérianne, Armand travels to Paris where his brother Edmond is pursuing his medical studies. The Paris of the two brothers is as different as their temperaments. While Armand's Paris is that of the poor, Edmond's city is that of his school, hospital, and the neighborhoods of the rich, the "Beaux Quartiers" of the right bank of the Seine:

Peaceful west, lined with trees, with well kept, lighted buildings, whose iron shutters permit the passage through their upper slits of joy and warmth, security, wealth. Oh! it is here that the carpets are thick and little barefoot girls run in long nightdresses because they do not want to sleep: life is so sweet and there will be company tonight if one can judge by the linen laid out, by the crystal service on a sideboard. The beaux quartiers . . . this long craft of luxury and peace sets up its lofty border with the gardens of the Trocadéro. . . . Then it is the affluent city, with anonymous streets, without commerce, with indistinguishable streets, white, like one another. . . . It goes up towards the north, it comes down towards the south, it goes the length of the Bois de Boulogne, it is cut with a few avenues, it displays squares like bouquets fastened to an expensive fur piece. . . . Les beaux quartiers. . . . It is like an escape from a nightmare in the black claw of industry. . . . Here slumber great ambitions, elevated thoughts, melancholies full of grace. . . . In these affluent surroundings, one would so like everything to be for the best in the best of all possible worlds. One dreams of forgetting, one dreams of loving, one dreams of living and one dreams of clinics and of works on which the angel of charity smiles. Life is an opera in the old style with its overtures, its ensembles, its great arias and the intoxication of violins. Les beaux quartiers.[20]

It is into the society of these *beaux quartiers* that Edmond resolves to enter and he does so by becoming the lover of a beautiful young woman, Carlotta, the mistress of the wealthy industrialist Joseph Quesnel. The elderly Quesnel has proposed this degrading arrangement in order to keep from losing Carlotta entirely. Thus does Edmond, in his entrance into society, choose the lot of the parasite in the parasitic world of the Quesnels, Wisners, and other members of the milieu to which we were introduced in *Les Cloches de Bâle*. Characters from this circle reappear from novel to novel in the manner of those in Balzac's "Comédie Humaine," playing larger or smaller roles. Joseph Quesnel, representing the syndicate that finally succeeded in breaking the strike of the Parisian taxi drivers in *Les Cloches de Bâle*, plays a more substantial role in *Les Beaux Quartiers*, while Wisner, the automobile magnate and lover of Diane de Nettencourt, whose financial manipulations figured so prominently in the first work, appears here only as another inhabitant of the *beaux quartiers*.

Joseph Quesnel, master of a vast financial domain, manipulator of governments, capable of incalculable baseness in his financial dealings, has fallen so deeply in love with Carlotta that he will do anything to keep her. There exists in him, as in every man, a multitude of conflicting personalities. The striking dissimilarity between the social and private personalities of men is a basic theme in Aragon's work. He refers to this phenomenon as that of the "double man." Quesnel describes this duality in a conversation with one of his business associates:

We are here and we talk together. And everything seems important to you. But you are in a hurry. Your mind is elsewhere. . . . Someone is waiting for you. . . . *I* speak to you. My lips move. I also have my lights and shadows. I also have within me a silent world. Government, business, numbers, all that is only a deceptive décor. I am thinking about what I do not say. We both probably hide a similar reality. . . . We are, like others, double men. We live in a historical period that will perhaps be characterized by that one day: the era of double men. I have always divided my life into two parts.[21]

The double man is at times so divided between the two facets of his nature that the private individual detests the public man who is so different from him. For Aragon, the true hero is one whose public life and private life are inseparable, one who makes no distinction between the two.

Edmond and Armand embody this duality in two individuals, with Edmond representing the immorality of the social man and Armand the morality of the private individual. It is Armand who follows Aragon's itinerary from the bourgeoisie to the Communist movement, who renounces his class to achieve solidarity with the proletariat. Aragon acknowledges his identity with Armand, as he did with Anicet, and quotes the Russian writer Fadeev to show that, whatever a writer talks about, whatever aspects of life he may reveal, he must in all his work include his own biography. Not only does such a concept of literature not contradict the Marxist-Leninist concept, but it is also from this position alone that it is possible to understand life properly and to awaken genuine feelings in man.[22]

Armand's life expresses the drama of certain men about whom Marx and Engels spoke in a passage of the *Communist Manifesto*. These men, at a particular moment of history, pass from their class, the bourgeoisie, to the rising class in which they see incarnated the future of all humanity, the proletariat. This drama, stated Aragon, is not simple, not without relapses, doubts, scruples, and heartbreak.[23] Armand rejects his background to become the modern hero, the Communist, a man who has had such insight into the world that he cannot forget it and for whom nothing henceforth can measure up to that revelation.

Armand's denunciation of the hypocrisy of modern bourgeois society is not without precedent in Aragon's work. As early as 1921, he wrote, in *Anicet ou le Panorama roman*, that the world was governed by minds that reasoned only on the basis of their own hypotheses. It was the period of elegant solutions. No one even questioned the formula of art for art's sake, but inscribed it like any other on the pediments of public buildings. To become a great man, it was only necessary to learn the proper formula.[24] Anicet had reached the point at which he was able to question the organization of capitalist society, which he had been taught was immutable and which he now perceived to be purely arbitrary. In *Le Paysan de Paris*, Aragon described how this arbitrary order was established: "There is in the world an unbelievable disorder, and what is most extraordinary is that as a rule men have sought, beneath the appearance of disorder, a mysterious order which is so natural to them, which expresses merely a desire existing within them, an order which they have no sooner introduced into things than one sees them marvel at this order and find an idea behind this order and then explain this order by an idea."[25]

Armand finally repudiates the existing order after one final attempt to adapt to it. One day, he meets Adrien Arnaud, who has continued his strike-breaking activities in Paris. He obtains a job for Armand as a scab worker in the Wisner automobile factory which is on strike. Armand experiences the joy of working for his own sustenance, but underlying his joy is the knowledge that he is still on the side of those who steal from, divide, and betray the people. The next day, breaking definitively with his family and with his class, he goes to the strike committee of the union of automobile workers, stating that he no longer wants to be a scab, but wants to join them. The workers, overwhelmed with despair at the failure of their strike, look at him with renewed faith. Then a man rises, throws his cap on the table, and exclaims in the ringing tones on which all of Aragon's novels end: "Comrades . . . you see that one must indeed never despair."[26]

IV Les Voyageurs de l'impériale (1942)

The title of this third volume of "Le Monde réel"[27] symbolizes the division of mankind into two races of men, those who wish only to preserve their comfort, and those who seek their destiny. "I thought that this impériale [outside platform of the bus], or rather the bus itself, represented a fair metaphor of life. For there are two kinds of people in the world, those who, like the people on the platform, are carried along without any knowledge of the machine they inhabit, and the others who know what makes the wheels go round, who manipulate the machinery of the monster. . . . And the former can understand nothing about the latter, because from the platform one can only look at the cafés, the street lamps, and the stars."[28]

In a newspaper interview, Aragon explained that his purpose in writing Les Voyageurs de l'impériale was to follow Les Beaux Quartiers with another picture of the decadence of the French bourgeoisie, to show how individualism leads to the degradation of the human being and to collective crime.[29] The protagonist of this novel, Pierre Mercadier, is patterned after Aragon's grandfather. Since childhood, Pierre had been preoccupied with the stock market, which had been discussed constantly in his home. The stock market was the barometer of social stability. Pierre believed that, while one could not have confidence in what one read in the newspapers, one could gain great insight into public affairs by reading the stock market quotations, since figures did not lie. In the course of his studies, he had come across the name of the Scottish financier John Law. Upon the death of Louis XIV, the finances of France were in a critical state, and Law succeeded in winning the support of the Regent for a scheme which promised quick returns for the treasury. He believed that the providing of credit and the issuance of paper money would stimulate trade and thus regenerate the French economy. Pierre's interest in John Law and in the effect of economics on the historical process was unusual at a time when history was taught as the struggle of the spirit of invention and progress against the spirit of tradition and reaction. At the beginning of his career as a professor of history, Pierre had written a short article on John Law for an academic journal and, for the rest of his life, gathered notes for the book he was never to write.

Pierre's preoccupation with money led him into various speculative ventures. First, he bought works of art by promising artists, but his wife's recriminations caused him to abandon this practice. Instead, he began to invest secretly in the stock market. His pleasure in gambling was doubled by the secrecy of these operations which became a means of deceiving his wife. Even the loss of one hundred thousand francs in the bankruptcy of the Panama Canal Company did not deter him from continued speculation. Indeed, his financial manipulations were the only thing that distracted him from his acute boredom with his students and with his family.

One day, he had a revelation that explained life to him. He discovered that all of the sentiments that seem to link us to others can be reduced to one thing, money. "There are no sentiments, there is only money. What ties Pierre to Paulette is money. If he cannot leave her, it is because of the complex problem such a move would entail, a problem that has nothing to do with love. And in what way is he indispensable to his children except in the relationship money created between them? That presents itself with all the idealistic outward appearances of duty, responsibility, affection, ties of blood, of love. . . . But, what is real, is money by which the father and husband provides for his family."[30]

Fortified with this knowledge, Pierre abandons his wife and children to seek a new life. He travels first to Venice where his mentor, John Law, spent the last three years of his life, supporting himself by gambling. From Venice, he travels to Monte Carlo where he gambles away his savings, and returns to Paris penniless and aged, to teach in a private school there. He accidentally meets his grandson, to whom he becomes attached, but is felled by a stroke before he can develop the relationship. Cared for until his death by an elderly, grotesque brothel keeper who has fallen in love with him, he dies in August, 1914, the date symbolizing the end of the old world. Just before he dies, he tries desperately to utter a word he never uttered in his lifetime, "politics."

It is by the desperate emptiness and solitude of Pierre's life that Aragon attempts to teach a lesson. By showing Pierre's alienation, Aragon seeks to arouse within the reader a desire for communion with his fellow man.

Pierre is defeated because he has never known "this link between days, this interest in someone that gives meaning to life."[31] Pascal, his son, remarks that it was his father's egotistical search for individual liberty that imprisoned his children. As Pascal goes off to war, he states that it was his father and men like him who led him there "with their blindness, their superb disdain of politics, their way of extricating themselves and leaving others in the mess."[32] For four years and three months, Pascal fights, "he no longer had any thoughts of his own, he was a part of an enormous body, of a wounded, roaring beast. He was waging war. He had shared the torments and the hopes of millions of other men like him."[33] From time to time, he thinks of his father and shrugs his shoulders at his egotistical individualism, knowing that the time of all the Pierre Mercadiers has gone by definitively. The theme of personal evasion, which had been so popular in the literature at the beginning of the twentieth century, and which Aragon had attacked in *Le Traité du style*, is discredited completely in this novel.

There appears at this time in Aragon's work a preoccupation with the passage of time and with old age. "One fine day the future is named the past/It is then that one turns around and sees his youth,"[34] wrote Aragon in *Le Nouveau Crève-coeur*. It is in *Les Voyageurs de l'impériale*, also written after his fortieth birthday, that this anguish is expressed so acutely that it almost assumes physical proportions in the minute, clinical descriptions of aging and decay: "Great, well-formed, huge tears, heavy, slow, long tears, rolled into the hair on the cheeks, were crushed near the mouth. Never had he felt so keenly how feeble age had made his arms, his legs without suppleness, his whole body emptied, skin rolling over ribs without muscles, the belly misshapen and swollen. The asthma in his chest was mixed with his suffering."[35] Pierre's physical deterioration is depicted as the external manifestation of his moral decay. There is only one weapon available to man in his battle against time and death and that is communion with a loved one, the first step in the direction of communion with a collectivity. Only by becoming an integral part of a collectivity that will live on after one's death can one triumph over time. *Les Communistes*, the long novel that follows and stems from "Le Monde réel," shows how individual despair can be assuaged by collective hope.

As in all of Aragon's work, there are many autobiographical elements in *Les Voyageurs de l'impériale*. Jeannot, Pascal's son, grows up in a pension run by his family, as did Aragon. Later on in life, he renounces his class to become a member of the Communist party. The foreign ladies who live in Pascal's pension, *L'Etoile-Famille*, are patterned after the ladies who used to shower the young Louis Aragon with candy and treats. When describing these ladies, Aragon interrupts the story to interject comments in his own name, a practice that becomes more and more frequent in his subsequent novels. At the *Etoile-Famille*, there were four Manescù ladies, a mother and three daughters, the wife and daughters of a M. Manescù, owner of a vast wheat-producing estate in Rumania. "Perhaps it is contrary to the rules of the novel and unfair to the reader to give here details about this austere person that anticipate events by five years, but it can't be helped," wrote Aragon. For, he continued,

without such perspective, one would look at this woman with less interest. It is thus not superfluous to know immediately that, when the Manescù ladies left Paris, there was no news of them for a few years because of international events. Then they learned from a post card from Rumania with a pretty stamp edged in violet that during a revolt, Mme Manescù's peasants had cut off her hands right at the wrists. That throws a certain light on the family and gives a certain ròmanticism to the person described. What makes you wonder are not so much the two stumps that one of the Manescù girls wrapped in the bottom of her petticoat which she had torn off in haste, but the fact that Mme Manescù had peasants. Belonging to her. Peasants. Who revolted. In Rumania. Where wheat grows. Who revolted because they were hungry. From time to time there is famine there. They became almost like crazy men. And they held this lady dressed in black responsible, with the white hands. Both hands. Cric, crac. But let us not anticipate any more.[36]

V   Aurélien (*1944*)

Aurélien, the protagonist of the fourth volume of "Le Monde réel" is another representative of bourgeois individualism. Like the other volumes in the series, *Aurélien*, in the manner of the traditional novel, tells a story. Autobiographical elements are mixed with fiction. In *J'Abats mon jeu*, Aragon wrote that Aurélien possessed certain of his characteristics and also some qualities of Drieu la Rochelle. His principal aim in this novel, however, was to give a picture of a man of his generation whose intellectual and moral formation were determined by World War I.

Aurélien had lost his youth in the war. He was a member of the class which had completed its three years of military service just at the beginning of the war and then had proceeded directly to the trenches for four more years. "Neither the dangers, nor the girls . . . had left an imprint on his heart. He had neither loved nor lived. He had not died, that was already something, and at times he looked at . . . his young body, his intact body, and he trembled, in retrospect, at the idea of the war cripples, his comrades, those one saw in the streets, those who would never return."[37]

After the war, he returns to civilian life, to a world that has changed. Since he has an income which frees him from the necessity of working, his life lacks direction, and he spends his days seeking ways in which to fill them. The central scene in the novel is a banquet of veterans of Aurélien's division who meet to share their regrets and disappointments. Forgetting the horror of the war, they look back on it with nostalgia. When they sing, a doctor who has known Aurélien only in civilian life, looks at him with astonishment. This distinguished young man, whom he has seen in the most elegant salons of Paris, always well dressed and silent, has only here been able to relax, for only with his former war comrades does he feel completely at ease.

Aurélien has begun to regret the war because he left behind him in the trenches his dreams of a human fraternity, a fraternity he now realizes is impossible. Since nothing now links him to society, he seeks a great love to give meaning to his life. He finds this passion in the person of Bérénice, a cousin of Edmond Barbentane (*Les Beaux Quartiers*), who has come from the provinces to visit Paris. Even before meeting Bérénice, Aurélien had been drawn to the name with its resonances of Barrès' *Le Jardin de Bérénice* and of Racine's heroine who symbolizes the power of love. Bérénice stands out in the circle of the Wisners, Barbentanes, and Quesnels. Aurélien notices that, in this society of postwar Paris, she is the only one who acts without artifice. She cannot be compared to any other woman he has ever met but reminds him of the "unknown woman of the Seine," a young woman who had been carried to a watery grave and whose death mask adorns his wall. As Aurélien's love for Bérénice grows, he notices an ever increasing resemblance between her and the death mask.

The love of Aurélien and Bérénice is hopeless in the society in which they live. Bérénice refuses to compromise and accept what passes for love among her contemporaries. She is driven by a desire for perfection, devoured by the passion for an absolute that burned within the Surrealists and which, according to Aragon, is so consuming that it cannot be described: "It devours those who look upon it. All those who have tried it are ensnared by it. You cannot try it and then change your mind. One trembles to name it: it is the taste for the Absolute. . . . It is the absence of resignation. If one desires, one can take pride in what it has done for mankind, for the sublime things to which this exigency has given rise. . . . He who has a taste for the Absolute renounces all happiness by that very fact. What happiness can resist this dizzyness, this constantly renewed need? "[38]

When Bérénice meets Aurélien, she is seeking the Absolute in a relationship with another human being, but Aurélien is incapable of comprehending her desire for perfection. He is able to love only in his own limited way. His love is serving a purpose, that of filling his days and justifying his existence. When Bérénice discovers that their love is impossible, she declares that it was really over before it began, "because it would have had to be so elevated, so great, so perfect, to be, simply to be . . ."[39] After Bérénice's departure, Aurélien returns to the meaningless life he had been leading, only now its very emptiness becomes intolerable to him. Love had succeeded in hiding the void, but now he is filled with great shame. He discovers that he was spared the enemy's bullet to face something much worse, self-contempt.

Paralleling the central theme of the love of Aurélien and Bérénice are the sordid adventures and intrigues of Edmond Barbentane and his circle. Edmond, who is now married to Quesnel's daughter, has been involved in various financial schemes in an effort to obtain some of his wife's money. He persuades Aurélien to invest in one of his ventures, in which Aurélien loses a considerable portion of his inheritance. He finds that he is unable to continue to lead the life he has been leading and agrees to leave Paris to work in the factory of his brother-in-law in Lille. Although he realizes that he is no longer in love with Bérénice, his relationship with her has left him with a certain longing for perfection.

The novel was to have ended with Aurélien's acceptance of bourgeois life. However, while writing *Aurélien*, Aragon was taking notes on the military events he saw going on about him as well as the exodus from Paris. The war, surrender, and occupation aroused within Aragon the desire to link *Aurélien*, the book of his past, with the present. For this reason, Aragon added an epilogue which takes place sixteen years later. Aurélien, who has married and had children in the interim, is a captain in the French army. He receives orders to proceed to the town of R., the town in which Bérénice lives with her husband. As he approaches R., Aurélien realizes that Bérénice has never left his heart. He loves his wife, she is his mature love, but Bérénice is his youth and what has survived in him of his youth. Although he had known Bérénice for only two months, those two months had, in truth, represented all of his youth.

Aurélien finds a Bérénice who has taken the step Catherine was unable to take, a Bérénice who has sheltered Spanish republicans, a Bérénice more preoccupied with the defeat of her beloved country than with reminiscing about their former love, a Bérénice who cries out that the French should never have surrendered, but should have defended their country to the end. Aurélien is astonished by the transformation. "I left a little passionate girl, spontaneous, ignorant of the world, ah, so profoundly foreign to this world in which men fight, oppose each other, throw themselves to the forefront of ideas, ideas which scarcely hide self-interest, intrigues . . . and then, I find again a woman who brings the same passion that she gave to life ... to these soiled ... hazy things ... to those things that were our sickness."[40] Aurélien then asks Bérénice why she is harboring Spanish republicans. When she replies that she does so because of their misfortunes, Aurélien states that the misfortune of those who are in the wrong can only be construed as justice. Bérénice reminds him that that is exactly what the Germans must be saying about their misfortune and adds that their visions of the world are more divergent than ever. All they have accomplished by this reunion, she maintains, is to tarnish their memories. As they return to her home, she is killed by a German bullet. Bérénice, however, has completed the journey Catherine was unable to finish, to become the prototype of the women of the future, the women who become the heroines of the long novel *Les Communistes.*

VI   Les Communistes

In two volumes of essays entitled *L'Homme Communiste*, Aragon extols the new hero of modern times, a man who is no longer a remote figure, but one who is accessible to all. This hero is a militant Communist and is morally superior to other heroes, just as the proletariat is morally superior to other classes. Aragon describes the characteristics of this new hero and attempts to capture the processes by which a man is modified to finally arrive at that stage of his evolution, which is called Communist man. In the second volume, Aragon describes four representatives of this new man, Jean-Richard Bloch, Paul Eluard, Jacques Duclos, and Maurice Thorez. The counterpart of Communist man, Communist woman, is not celebrated in these volumes, but receives her apotheosis in the six volumes of *Les Communistes*, published from 1949 to 1951. According to Aragon, the title should be read as written in the feminine, since it was in the hands of women that a great share of the honor of France remained alive during the shameful years of the French defeat and occupation. It was women who rebuilt the Communist party after it was outlawed at the time of the German-Soviet pact. The subtitle of the work, "The Novel of France," was added by Aragon to indicate that there is no individual protagonist; the protagonist is the entire French nation.

The prologue to the first volume depicts the exodus of the republicans from Spain after their defeat. It ushers in the rest of the novel, just as the Spanish Civil War ushered in the larger war. The remainder of the work deals with the period from February, 1939 to June, 1940. Volume I centers on the Russo-German nonagression pact and the reactions to it in the business community. Aragon describes how the Fascists in France profit from the pact and then traces the reactions to it of the French Communists. Volume II deals with the lull before the fighting, during which the British and French troops awaited the arrival of the German army. The author shows how those in power think only of their wealth and profits, while the generals dream of campaigns against the Russians. The Communist party is dissolved by the government and reconstituted clandestinely. The third volume deals with the meeting of January 16, 1940 of the Chambre des Députés, now the only legal means of expression left to the Communists. Volume IV centers on the rivalry between the politicians Reynaud and Daladier; the two volumes of book five portray the invasion, exodus, and debacle of May 10 to June 10, 1940.

Historical characters appear throughout these volumes and are interspersed with fictional characters, many of whom figured in the earlier novels of "Le Monde réel." The new fictional characters are young people in their twenties who belong to a different generation. Aragon wanted to oppose this generation of the French defeat to the generation of the French victory of 1918. By comparing and contrasting men like Aurélien with the young Jean de Moncy, or Cécile with Bérénice, he was seeking to point out certain national types that emerged from both wars. He also wanted to show the final stages in the decline of the bourgeoisie, a class that he believed preferred the German occupation to the possibility of another Commune.

Les Communistes is not really a novel; it is a panoramic tract which gives the effect of a series of newspaper reports, editorials, and party speeches. None of the characters is dealt with in depth. There is no psychological analysis of the characters, a technique which is frowned upon in Marxist literature. There are instead portraits of various members of different social classes, with emphasis on party members. The reactions of all of the characters are determined by their economic and social backgrounds. There are, however, two people, Cécile d'Aigrefeuille and Jean de Moncy, who emerge from the multitude. The interweaving of their destinies constitutes a thread which runs through the six volumes. Cécile, a member of the privileged circle of Aurélien and Edmond Barbentane, marries Fred Wisner, the handsome nephew of the automobile magnate. She begins to sense the ugliness underlying the polished manners of members of her class, including her husband and father. Because she has an intuition of something better, she is disturbed to discover that the men of her class are dominated by their interest in maintaining and increasing their wealth and privileges at any cost. Her groping takes concrete form only after she meets the brother of her personal maid, who has been blinded and lost his hands in the fight against the Germans. Joseph Gigoux teaches her what it is to be a Communist. Were he not one, his personal tragedy would have been unendurable, but he is saved by the party, which provides him with a goal in life and a justification for his continued existence. If personal affairs occupy an enormous role in the life of a man, and the personal life is destroyed, then it becomes a catastrophe and the victim no longer desires to live. But the militant Communist is never faced with this problem. Joseph Gigoux illustrates this concept for Cécile:

> ... what was I, a worker like any other, I could have been killed or lost a limb in an accident—what meaning would that have had? ... While, now, for the price of my eyes and my arms, what have I bought? I am going to tell you. Now, I am a severely wounded war cripple. And, later, and perhaps that won't be very far off, when there are demonstrations, since I still have legs, I will walk in front, and the police will not be able to fire on me, or it will cause a great uproar! And my comrades will pass with me ... when one thinks about it, a man even as damaged as I can still serve."[41]

Gigoux embodies Aragon's concept of the hero of modern times, who wants only to serve the cause of mankind. "He can fight for the happiness of others, since he finally knows that happiness is not a chimera, that it exists, that it is worth all sacrifices, and that one can give it to another."[42] And this is the justification for life, making happiness possible ". . . for the human species, that extraordinary precious thing, which tears itself apart, and seems to be afraid of its own growth, of its future of light and greatness."[43]

Despite the horrors and injustice described in *Les Communistes*, this work is basically optimistic. It contains none of the despair of contemporary existentialist works in which man finds himself pitted against a hostile, meaningless universe, which constantly crushes him. The symbol of this modern anguish is Sisyphus, eternally condemned by the Gods to push his heavy rock up the hill, in full knowledge of the fact that it will only roll down again. The Marxist universe is not an existentialist but a manichean universe, in which the forces of light are pitted against the forces of darkness, which they will eventually defeat to ensure a better world. The Marxist world has a structure. It is no longer an absurd universe without laws, but an objective one in which each action has a clear meaning. Marxist literature gives primacy to the real world and the banal details of everyday life and makes all of this significant by interpreting it in the light of a predetermined movement of history. Metaphysical anguish gives way to social progress.

While the teachings of Joseph Gigoux alter the ideas Cécile has received from her class, her love for Jean de Moncy opens up a new world for her. Jean, too, is transformed by his love. Before meeting Cécile, he is completely alienated from society. He is neither attached to any belief nor motivated by any passion. His only heroes have been heroes of flight and evasion, like Rimbaud. He slowly takes the path taken in *Les Beaux Quartiers* by Armand Barbentane, who appears again in *Les Communistes*, mobilized for the second time. A revealing, autobiographical detail is given by Aragon when he speaks about Armand, stating that when a man comes to the Communist party from the working class, he can devote all of his energy to fighting the class enemy. Armand, on the other hand, has to constantly divert some of his energy to combat a part of himself that survives from his bourgeois past and which he hates, but fears constantly that he does not hate enough.

In one of the essays included in the collection *J'Abats mon jeu*, Aragon states that he was extremely objective in *Les Communistes*. He cites in support of this contention his sympathetic treatment of non-Communists like Colonel Avoine and the fictional Father Blomet, who demonstrates unparalleled heroism in the struggle against the Germans. Aragon felt that his objectivity was particularly difficult, since *Les Communistes* was the book about the martyrdom of France. It documented the blood bath for the men of his country, whose perils and griefs he had shared. Aragon's extensive historical documentation came from many sources, including his own experiences as a member of a unit that had covered the entire front from the entrance of French troops into Belgium in May to the rout at Dunkirk in June, 1940.

The author's claim to objectivity is open to doubt in the light of his attempts to prove in this novel that the interests of France coincided with the interests of Russia at the time of the Russo-German pact: When Pierre Cormeilles, a Communist professor, explains the pact, he says that if French interest does not appear to coincide with Russian interest, it is only because one is unable to see how it does coincide in reality, and that one must consider the matter from a dialectical point of view. The exemplary characters in the novel are those who never question the actions of the party. Those who do raise objections are characterized as Trotsky-ites or cops. Throughout *Les Communistes*, Aragon faithfully adheres to party dogma. He condones the Russian occupation of the Baltic countries and aggression against Finland, but attacks the Allied decision to mine Norwegian waters to stop iron shipments to Germany during the time of the Russo-German pact. Because Aragon is more interested in this work in defending a thesis than in telling a story, he has sacrificed the novel to the political tract. The characters are not alive, but remain merely two-dimensional incarnations of Aragon's principles.

VII   La Semaine sainte (Holy Week)

This novel was published in 1958 to universal critical acclaim. Critics who had ignored or discounted Aragon's previous work because of his political sympathies praised what they termed his return to objectivity. *Holy Week* recounts the events that took place during Easter Week of 1815, from the first news of Napoleon's escape from Elba to the breakup of the entourage of Louis XVIII on the Belgian border. At the time the novel opens, Napoleon is moving toward Paris and his band of one thousand men has been growing into an army. In Paris, on Palm Sunday, the sick, gouty king declares that he will defend Paris and, should it be necessary, die in defense of the people. After crying that he will never abandon his people, he takes off under cover of night for the Belgian border. With him go the nobles, their families and servants, and seven thousand musketeers and guards. Most of the hundreds of characters surrounding the king are historical persons and include two future kings of France, Charles X and Louis Philippe, the "bourgeois king," as well as generals, officers and soldiers. Step by step, Aragon shows the disintegration of the king's entourage: "An army must be someone's army. They were no longer the army of the people they were abandoning. They were no longer defending anything, merely defending themselves against the wind, the wind occupied them, twisted in them as in the well of a staircase."[44] The flight ends on the eve of Easter Sunday with a few hundred bedraggled horsemen making their way into Belgium with the king.

The exodus is described through the eyes of many characters. It was not only the king and his entourage that Aragon wanted to portray, but also those who, often mutely, watched them pass, the people in their houses and the poor along the road, "the people in a word, the people of that time from whom emerged the people of today, and whom novelists as a rule have neglected until the present."[45] The action of the novel comes from the encounter between the king's party and the people with whom they come in contact in the course of their retreat. The central view is that of the painter Théodore Géricault, who accompanies the royal retreat as a musketeer of the king. Aragon chose Géricault as the focal point of the novel because he was a painter of the people, one of the first painters of the working man, who occupies the same place in painting as Stendhal does in literature.

The basic theme of this vast work is the artist, his discovery of the meaning of loyalty and his discovery of the people of his nation. Géricault begins the week without any great feelings of loyalty. During the course of the week, on Ash Wednesday, he inadvertently is witness to a conspiratorial meeting of radical French groups to which he is brought by a jealous suitor. By revealing the plot of these radicals to a musketeer of the king, the young man seeks to destroy his rival, one of the leaders of the conspiracy. Hidden in a thicket, Géricault discovers a world he never knew existed, the world of the people. Gathered here with no common ground except their hunger, suffering, and misery, these men reveal to Géricault "a swarming of destinies deprived of hope. Where did they live, what were their women like, what monstrous prices did they pay for the bread about which they spoke with an anxiety so novel to Théodore? "[46] Géricault discovers the humanity of these people, just as Cécile (*Les Communistes*) discovered that her maid lived and suffered as she did, that she had an existence other than that devoted to serving Cécile. For the first time, Géricault sees the world objectively. Although he hardly understood the language these people were speaking, he wanted to help them. "How could he join his strength, his breath, his soul to their fever? They were *the others*: and that was the laceration, the physical pain, *the others*."[47]

Like Catherine Simonidzé, Géricault is unable to take the decisive step required to enter the world of tragedy he has just discovered. He does, however, discover something that exists within him of which he had been unaware, something that would forever after remain a part of him; his sympathy made him one of them:

Nothing any longer appeared the same to him. Every wretched house, every man in the fields, every farm hand, every headdress, every petticoat that stole away at the soldiers' approach—they were to him as though he were touching with his finger an unknown, yet discovered reality. He no longer looked on passers-by, on a crowd, as such; every human being assumed a meaning, a life of his own. He thought with something akin to anger of those painters who in their landscapes would leave to any nobody the painting of the little figures with which they would strew them conventionally. The slightest outline of a human form conveyed to him the substance of a being. A being of flesh and blood like himself. How was it that this simple idea had not come to him sooner? He had of course known it in the abstract. . . . But even so. He had not known it, really known it.[48]

Géricault's feelings are those experienced by Aragon near Saarbrücken that night in 1919 when he realized that the German workers, on whom he was instructed to fire, were in the right. That, for Aragon, was the decisive moment, the moment in which he discovered *the others*:

Because, as a matter of fact, all this has to do not with Théodore's life, but with mine. Don't you recognize it? Nothing of this could have occurred in 1815, don't you see? The sources are obvious. My life is my life. Not only Voelklingen in 1919, not only that. My whole life. The way I have of roaming the world, discovering 'strange crafts in their every detail, how a horse is shod, how a sword is forged. . . . This people. disunited, divided, the poorest not knowing which way to turn, acting against their manifest interest. The lack of an ideology. The time it will take for all this to work itself out, or to seem to work itself out.[49]

When speaking about the wealth of historical detail included in *Holy Week*, Aragon stated that he undoubtedly recounted events in too minute detail. He did so because he was unable to give free rein to his imagination without having reality as a point of departure. After re-creating the historical atmosphere, he then proceeded to breathe life into the novel by inventing, or by prevaricating. Aragon believes that the very art of the novel consists of knowing how to invent. He confesses that he brought such great attention to minute details in the setting and took such care to restore it as it was, to make the reader more disposed to believe in his characters. By fidelity to details that can be verified, the artist is able to succeed in his prevarications. There is nothing like truth to serve as an introduction to a lie. Therefore, concluded Aragon, "believe me when I say that this is not a historical novel, but an impudent exploitation of history which I have made a stepping stone to the fiction, a passport to the novel."[50]

Aragon's choice of a painter as the center of his novel is in keeping with the constant interest he has shown in that medium of artistic expression. As early as *Anicet*, he had his hero express his jealousy of the art of Bleu/Picasso, which he regarded as superior to his. It is perhaps also because of his fascination with painting that Aragon excels in images of a visual nature. In *L'Homme Communiste*, he compared war-torn France to Géricault's famous painting, the *Raft of the Medusa*, which shows tormented, suffering people adrift without compass or direction on a terrifying sea. "At that time France was a raft adrift carrying shipwrecked people, and food was lacking, the children were pale, the women rent the heavens with their cries, men so thin that one could see their suffering, fixed the curse of their dry eyes on expanses without sails . . . you can at your leisure complete the allegory of the new Medusa."[51]

The education Géricault acquires about his country in the course of the exodus is paralleled by the deepening of his artistic vision. Géricault had matured during Napoleon's wars and had joined the musketeers because he found Louis XVIII more glamorous than this eternal warrior. His first disillusionment comes when the king leaves Paris. As he progresses on his journey, he realizes that the king, who welcomes foreign intervention, is no better than Napoleon with his endless wars. Neither one promises a better future for his country. Géricault decides that when he returns to painting he will paint neither court nor battle scenes, but will attempt to reproduce reality. Even before the events of this Holy Week, Géricault had expressed his admiration for Caravaggio's painting, in particular his *Death of the Virgin*, whom the master chose to represent "not as a princess on her canopied bed with a graceful curtain arrangement," but as a "woman of the people, marked by the whole process of the death agony, the sweat which has not been wiped away, the discoloration of the nostrils, the pallor of the flesh, the traces of pain, the body deformed by illness."[52] It was the insights gained during this Holy Week that made Géricault understand that Caravaggio's vision could not be limited to esthetics. Caravaggio's painting transcribed life, it was an affirmation of *the others*, as they had revealed themselves to Géricault that night at Poix. The opposition of light and shadow employed by Caravaggio was a means, not an end.

The concentrated time scale of one week, starting on Palm Sunday and ending on the eve of Easter Sunday, is used to encompass a multitude of flash-backwards and flash-forwards, a technique which Aragon calls stereoscopic and which he employs exclusively in his later novels *La Mise à mort* and *Blanche ou l'oubli*. While the result of this technique provides for an episodic and fragmentary novel, it reflects the basic chaos of life. It also shows the interdependence of the past, present, and future, each of which explains and gives meaning to the other.

Perhaps I have picked up this strange old damask of history, assisted by doubts and certainties, following the crisscross threads of the fabric, the complex tapestry of men and colors; perhaps I have flung myself into the crown of a vanished time in order to break away from that simplified, linear vision of the world in which I am completing a trajectory, to seek in the dust the multiple seeds of what I am, of what we are, and especially of what will spring from us, against us, above us, beyond us, that springtime of cemeteries which we call the future. Perhaps it is because at this moment I measure the limited present that is still allotted to me, that with all my strength, with all my will power, with a mad labor which makes those about me shake their heads, I have foolishly undertaken to divert all the past toward the future.[53]

Aragon believes that man is turned not toward the past, but toward the future, and he is certain that "at the supreme moment, when it is borne in upon the flesh how cruelly brief that very moment is, the soul looks forward, yearns to know more, and seeks with the feeble strength of an eye whose light is failing to guess what lies ahead, beyond the turn in the road, the new horizon . . . the future."[54] Beyond the turn of the road, for the Communist, lies a new world. Aragon defined the Communist as a man whose belief in human progress is at the basis of his concept of the world. This belief in human progress contradicts those critics who regarded *Holy Week* as a departure either from Aragon's political ideology or from the doctrine of Socialist Realism. In *J'Abats mon jeu*, Aragon wrote that *La Semaine sainte* was a logical development from *Les Communistes*, that both works were documented in the same way, and that if he had not at first had the experience of describing the war of 1940, he would have been unable to describe the movements of the entourage of King Louis XVIII. He said that he would never have been able to understand the soldiers of Napoleon and of Louis XVIII if he had not first served in Foch's army, as did Aurélien, and in the 1940 army of the pitiful Gamelin, as did Armand Barbentane and Jean de Moncy. It is true that the role played by the imagination was greater in *Holy Week* than in *Les Communistes*, where his documentation was made at first hand. Still, *Holy Week* could only have been written by a Communist, Aragon maintained, since it was researched and documented in accordance with the requirements of Socialist Realism. Aragon visited the city of Saint-Denis, just as he visited the places that figured in *Les Communistes*, to seek beneath its modern façade the old city of gardens, industries, canals, and windmills, through which the characters of *Holy Week* were to pass. A certain "poetry" emanating from the city took hold of him and, instead of the three or four pages he contemplated devoting to that city, he wrote more than fifty pages on Saint-Denis.

Historical documentation is an essential part of Socialist Realism and must not be construed as applicable only to a somewhat remote period in time. All of his characters are historical, according to Aragon, since they are indissolubly linked to their time, and all of his novels are historical, although not staged in period costume. While traditional novelists created characters patterned upon people who actually existed, Aragon does the opposite. Rather than give a fictitious name to the personality traits of a real person, he projects his own experiences and makes them part of a person with a historical name. While this person certainly did not have the thoughts Aragon attributes to him at a certain time, he might possibly have had them at some time in his life.

The conclusion of *Holy Week* optimistically proclaims Aragon's belief in the transformation of man and his future happiness. He expresses this belief by a reworking of the ancient Christian myths, which he had sought to destroy in his earlier works, in an effort to make way for the new, modern mythology. In *La Peinture au défi* of 1930, Aragon maintained that attacking symbols was not a childish undertaking, but an important step forward. "There is reason to hope that . . . a handful of fanatics will cause the disappearance of all illusions to the infamous cross. . . . Today the most beautiful painting in the world, if it represents a religious subject, is incomprehensible to me as a painting. The subject hides it. I would prefer to it the most stupid and most inanimate still life."[55] Later on, in his wartime poetry, Aragon returned to the old Christian myths and made use of them, together with pagan and modern myths. He did this in an effort to make his works more accessible to a vast public and also because he had learned to respect his Catholic companions in the Resistance. In *Holy Week*, Aragon again uses the old Christian myths but gives to them a modern interpretation, as he describes the midnight tolling of the church bells before the Easter Sunday that was to conclude Holy Week of 1815:

It is not the Angel of the Lord who has descended from heaven with a great trembling of the earth, who has rolled away the stone and seated himself upon it. The one whose countenance here is like lightning, the one whose raiment is not white as snow, is Man, and let those who bear the sword gaze upon him and tremble! Man is reborn, the keepers have fled, life begins again, the life of every day where there is no need for anyone to perform miracles, where a glass and a knife sing like a canticle on a table, a woman's hand suffices to make light at the curtain that she draws aside, and little violin players walk on country roads, picking blackberries in the hedges . . . [56]

Holy Week differs from the earlier novels and anticipates Aragon's later novels *La Mise à mort* and *Blanche ou l'oubli*, since here he shows his characters not only in action, but also dreaming. To external description and conversation, he has added stream of consciousness. The juggling of the three dimensions of time—past, present, and future—in *La Semaine sainte*, *La Mise à mort*, and *Blanche ou l'oubli* differs from the technique employed in the earlier novels of "Le Monde réel," where Aragon told his stories chronologically.

Aragon has never limited his novels to a mere re-creation of the past or a description of the present. He has attempted in all of his work, especially in his novels, to express his ideas and teach his philosophy. He has failed when his vision has been too greatly affected by his political bias and has succeeded, as he did in *La Semaine sainte*, when his political intent has not subverted his artistic genius.

CHAPTER 5

The Love of Elsa and the Great Poetic Works

I *"Elsa, I Love You"*

In a testimonial to the transcendence of love, Aragon wrote: ". . . look at me, perhaps I am a madman, perhaps a slave, perhaps a fool, but I say this to you, I have learned but one thing in this life, I have learned to love. And I can wish you nothing more than to know how to love."[1] He has described many times the momentous meeting with Elsa in the café in Montparnasse:

> And you came in November and because of
> a few words
> My life suddenly changed completely
> One evening at the bar of the Coupole
>
> Before you I was but an unsatisfied shadow
> Wandering deaf and dumb
> You taught me everything light of my life
> Even how to see the color of the day
>
> You who reopened for me the heaven of
> righteousness
> Who awakened within me profound music
> You who made me what I am and told me
> to sing
>
> Like a child before the world[2]

After Aragon's marriage to Elsa Triolet, all of his work was dedicated to and inspired by her. It has been Elsa who has played the decisive role in the life of Aragon and, since 1940, his love for her has filled his poems. Only poetry, according to Aragon, is capable of expressing the magnitude of his love: ". . . all that I am, all that I have ever been, my heart, my life, my dreams, dispute the validity of an idea of poetry which considers the lyrical art as a minor activity. That art is for me the most elevated achievement of man, the justification of his existence."[3]

The impersonal woman of his early poems became Elsa. She is ever present in his poems, and every part of her is evoked in Aragon's verses. In "Amour d'Elsa," the images in the various stanzas fit together to form the entire figure of Elsa, her countenance, her hair, her neck, her body, her hands, and her feet. Elsa became the personification of love, to speak of love was to speak of her, to understand the day one had to see her sleep, and to understand the night it was necessary to sleep beside her.[4] All the beauties of life were encompassed in Aragon's love for his wife.

But his idyll was interrupted. At the beginning of the war, when his pattern of life had been so cruelly altered, when all the world was in chaos and no one knew what the next day would bring, he could cling to his love, the one unchanging thing in a disordered universe:

> Oh my love oh my love only you exist
> For me in this hour of sad twilight
> When I lose both the thread of my poem
> And the thread of my life and my voice and
>   my joy
> Because I wanted to tell you again that I
>   love you
> And that these words hurt when spoken without
>   you[5]

The war had separated him from his beloved, and he cried out in distress against this terrible isolation:

> Give me back give me back my sky and my
>   music
> My wife without whom all lacks song and
>   color
> Without whom May is but a deserted waste
>   for me
> The sun an insult and the shadow a
>   sorrow[6]

After he was reunited with his wife, he realized that he could not be happy while France was enslaved. The poem "There Is no Happy Love," written in 1943, expresses the impossibility of happiness in a world of misery and suffering:

> My beautiful love my dear love my wound
> I carry you within me like an injured bird
>
> . . . .
> Before one has the time to learn to live
>   it is already too late
> Then our hearts cry together in unison
>   in the night
> How much unhappiness goes into the
>   slightest song

How many regrets pay for a thrill
How many sobs are required for a song on a guitar
There is no happy love

There is no love that is not destined for suffering
There is no love which does not bruise
There is no love which does not blight
And the love of country as well as the love of you
There is no love that does not feed on tears
There is no happy love
But is is our love, ours[7]

Aragon has said that his having written that there is no happy love presupposes an exalted idea of the nature of true love. Love, he states, is not an exclusive, egotistical passion between two individuals, but one that embraces all of mankind, one that cannot accustom itself to inhumanity. When he wrote this poem, he also feared for Elsa's safety. During the war, directives were issued within the Resistance that couples engaged in clandestine activities had to separate for security reasons. Aragon asked Elsa to stop her activities so that they might remain together. She refused to sit by and be obliged to say "nothing," when asked at the end of the war what she had done. This refusal, wrote Aragon, destroyed within him those male prejudices which, "under the pretext of assuming all the responsibilities of the couple, confine woman to being merely a reflection of the male."[8]

"There Is no Happy Love" suggests also that love, no matter how perfect, is always threatened by the passage of time and by death. As early as *Aurélien*, Aragon described this basic sadness underlying every love as well as every human action: "Time goes along as if one had eternity before one; however, these days have a worm in the fruit: the never to be forgotten certainty of their end, the obsession with their brevity."[9]

The flight of time and the remembrance of past love is the theme of "Elsa je t'aime" ("Elsa I Love You"). This is a souvenir type of poem, reminiscent of the poems of the Romantic poets, in which the poet expressed his anguish at the flight of time and his desire to render his love immortal through his verses: "Beveled by every kiss/The years wear down too quickly/Avoid avoid avoid/Shattered memories."[10] The poet recalls the various places in which he and his beloved found happiness, and he protests against the swiftness of time's passage in the Lamartinian alexandrine: "Life will have flowed away without our noticing it."[11] He again laments the rapid flight of time in *Cantique à Elsa* (*Canticle to Elsa*), the first of a series of long, autobiographical poems:

> Never sated with these eyes for which I
> am starved
> My sky my despair my wife
> . . . .
> For thirteen years I have trembled on
> the doorstep of imagination
> Thirteen years of a bittersweet fear
> And for thirteen years invented
> imaginary perils
>
> Oh my child time is not to our measure
> A thousand and one nights are few for
> lovers
> Thirteen years are like a day and it is
> a fire of straw
> Which burns away at our feet thread by thread
> The magic carpet of our isolation[12]

Not only did Aragon idealize his own love in his war poetry, he also showed the perfect, unselfish love that was capable of every sacrifice in order to preserve the external conditions that had made this love possible. "La Dame de Chateaurenard" (*Le Crève-coeur*) is dedicated to Mathilde, the widow of the Resistance hero Gabriel Péri, who vainly waits at her window for a man who refused to accept a country of "men on their knees."

II Les Yeux d'Elsa

Les Yeux d'Elsa (*Elsa's Eyes*) carried the name of Aragon's beloved throught France and the anti-Fascist world:

> It came about that one beautiful evening the
> universe was shattered
> On reefs that the wreckers set afire
> I saw shining above the sea
> Elsa's eyes Elsa's eyes Elsa's eyes[13]

Through continual reiteration, Aragon wished to assure eternal life for his love by placing it in the tradition of the great loves of history, with Elsa taking her rightful place alongside of Helen of Troy, Petrarch's Laura, and Lamartine's Elvira:

> What if the boat of the stars capsizes
> Since it bears your name shake out the reefs
> They will see it shine on the great mast of
> the ship
> Then Helen Laura Elvira
> Will come out to greet you like a month of Mary[14]

Aragon turned for inspiration to the courtly love poetry of the twelfth century. In his devotion to his beloved, he compares himself to Lancelot, "the knight of the barrow/Who ignores what he fears when led by love."[15] While Aragon's concept of love was closely linked to that of courtly love which stressed the equality of woman, his poetry was distinguished from what preceded it, because his verses were written for his wife, while throughout history love poetry had been addressed to a mistress. One of the most famous genres of courtly poetry was the aubade, the morning song which announced the approach of dawn and the need for the lover to flee before discovery. But Aragon was singing of a conjugal love, peculiar to his time. In "Arma virumque cano," written in February, 1942, Aragon answered those who criticized his celebration of his love for his wife.

My love, they say that a man owes it to himself not to reveal his love in public. I answer that a man has nothing better, purer and more worthy of being perpetuated than his love, which is that very music about which Portia spoke, and that it is cowardice and weakness to fear to extol one's love. I want a day to come when, looking back at our night, people will see a flame that was shining there, and what flame can I revive but the one that is in me? My love, you are my only acknowledged family and I see the world through your eyes, it is you who make this universe tangible and who give meaning to human sentiments within me.[16]

In the poems of the war years, Aragon identified Elsa with France. The two loves illuminated each other and, at times, were fused into one great passion. So closely were they bound that, during those terrible days, "France and love cried the same tears."[17] Many were tempted to see Elsa as a symbol for France, but Aragon states that despite censorship, he spoke quite openly, and that when he spoke of Elsa, it was of his love, a creature of flesh and blood and not a myth. It was his love for Elsa that inspired him to sing of his love for his country. It was she who told him,

> If you want me to love you bring me pure
>   water
> In which they may quench their thirst
> . . . .
> Let your poem be the hope that says To be
>   continued
> At the bottom of the dark serial of our
>   steps
> So that the human voice may triumph over
>   the brasses
>   And give a reason to live
> To those who find only reasons for death[18]

While Elvira and Laura were essentially myths in the verses of their poets, Elsa is a real person who shares Aragon's philosophic concepts.

As early as 1929, in a questionnaire on the subject of love in *La Révolution surréaliste*, Aragon wrote that he placed all of his hope in love and in revolution, which could not be separated from each other. When asked whether he would sacrifice his ideals for love, he replied that anything that required the sacrifice of all that constituted the dignity of life could not be called love. Later, he wrote that love was the prefiguration within the limits and dimensions of a human life of the happiness of mankind. In love, each one prefers the other to himself. This is the first step away from individualism toward collective hope which represents the basis for historical optimism.

III *The Couple*

Aragon's communion with Elsa led him to the concept of the couple as the embodiment of love in the twentieth century. The innovation in modern poetry, wrote Aragon, is that "man can no longer be conceived of without woman, or woman without man . . . that the lofty expression of modern love is no longer an *idea* . . . but the couple . . . when man and woman raise themselves simultaneously to the same concept of the world, in which their love broadens, grows and becomes identified with the future of mankind."[19] Since the couple presupposes equality between the partners, the first step in the rehabilitation of the couple was to free woman from bondage and place her in her rightful place alongside of man. It was this mission that Aragon undertook in *Les Cloches de Bâle*, one to which he has remained faithful throughout his life. While the first four volumes of "Le Monde réel" demonstrate the impossibility of the ideal couple in a bourgeois milieu dominated by money, *Les Communistes* presents a couple, Cécile and Jean, who are able to surmount many of the obstacles their predecessors were unable to overcome. There are also, in *Les Communistes*, examples of true couples in the working class. Young Micheline becomes active in clandestine party work when her husband is called back to his unit and forges thereby another profound, unbreakable link between them, "a sweet thing that is not expressed aloud, a secret of love, their love and the love of all, a caress of the heart, the negation of solitude, of shadow and fear . . ."[20]

"What is the worth of a man alone" asks Aragon in *Les Communistes*, and the answer is that without a woman a man is "dust, an animal on the watch, or a sleeping stone."[21] It is woman who makes a man of him, and he distinguishes himself from the animals in the measure in which he is defined in relationship to a woman. The couple is the "principle of all moral movement, as well as of all physical mutations."[22] All of Aragon's poetry has been a profound meditation on the theme of the couple, "this sweetness of man and woman for whom the world is not limited as long as they are mingled, their breath and their bodies, their exaltation and their repose . . . their thoughts are interwoven like a braid of happiness; on all sides, they prolong themselves towards that future that is within them, and which can exist only through their rapprochement. . . . This experience cannot be transmitted. Those who have it experience at the same time the dizzyness and the marvelous intensity."[23] In *J'Abats mon jeu*, Aragon wrote that he envisaged communism as a society in which the basic cell would be the united couple of man and woman, faithful, happy and in love. Love is the only and final revelation of man's destiny. It is the criterion for judging the purity and profundity of the soul, and its didactic virtues are incontestable in poetry and novels. Aragon's own life can be divided into two periods, the one preceding and the one subsequent to the formation of the couple, a division also made by Elsa in her life. "My past was *before we met*. The past we shared together is always present. The other past is the *past-alone*, the *past-imperfect*,"[24] wrote Elsa in the preface to one of the thirty-eight volumes in a series containing the complete combined works of Aragon and Elsa. Their works, crossing and interlacing from volume to volume, will maintain their identity as a couple, even in death: "When we finally lie dead side by side, the marriage of our works will unite us for better or for worse in that future that was our dream and our main preoccupation, both yours and mine."[25]

IV Les Yeux et la mémoire (Eyes and Memory)

In a series of long autobiographical poems, each one approximately five thousand lines in length, Aragon recounts in a variety of metric patterns and in verses ranging from lyric to epic, from satiric to elegiac, the story of his life, before and after his meeting with Elsa. All of these poems continue the glorification of Elsa, begun in *Cantique à Elsa* and *Les Yeux d'Elsa*, which culminates in her apotheosis in *Le Fou d'Elsa*.

Les Yeux et la mémoire (1954), the first of the series, derives its name from a verse of the poem, "Du Poète à son parti" ("From the Poet to His Party"), the concluding poem of *La Diane française*, where Aragon wrote that it was his party that had guided him in his struggle against the Germans by giving him visions of the future of France and memories of her past. This poem, written in fifteen cantos, was inspired by Elsa's novel *Le Cheval roux*, which had been published in 1953 in the shadow of the hydrogen bomb. Her book centers on the possibility of the destruction of humanity by the new weapons and the question of peace. It deals with the man of the future and how he will differ from the man of today, if humanity is indeed able to survive. The book opens with the dropping of the bomb, leaving a handful of survivors who are awaiting imminent death.

Aragon's poem, composed in counterpoint to this novel, reaffirms his love even in the face of the destruction of the world: "My love at the end of the world/Ah at least may my voice answer you."[26] He maintains that everything he writes is in response to Elsa and for her:

> If the songs end in smoke
> What does it matter that no one listens
> Steps are erased from roads
> I continue to rhyme them
> Through a sort of madness
> Answering you with a song
> My only echo my beloved[27]

Before he met her, he was only a "dissatisfied shadow," and now he begs her to

> Stay my happy and unhappy love
> Stay prisoner in my arms my love
> Secret sunshine of the heart that belongs only
>   to the two of us
> My dear only love my final love
>
> If only your name remains of what I have
>   written
> I will hail the eternal glory of things[28]

Their love and all loves are inextricably bound up with history:

> If the hearts of a man and woman are truly
>   united
> History and their love tie them tightly
>   together
> They hope together and despair together
> They stand erect together or fall on their
>   knees
>
> The couple is like a united people[29]

Throughout *Les Yeux et la mémoire*, events of the early 1950s such as the coup in Guatemala, the Geneva agreement on Indochina and the execution of Julius and Ethel Rosenberg, are intermingled with expres-

sions of Aragon's love for Elsa. Despite the horrors and suffering described, there is expressed in this poem hope and faith in the future of
mankind. "I sing of arms and the man," becomes here "I sing of man and
his peaceful goals."[30] For it is only in a peaceful universe that man and
woman will truly be able to love:

> Nothing makes man and woman as great
> As this love for each other that takes
>   hold of them
> Happy are they who will love one day
> In a different universe[31]

While Aragon continues to maintain that it is his party that gives promise
of a peaceful world of the future, a new note enters his work, expressing
the fatigue of the former militant who desires to dream a bit in his old age:

> Is it really a crime to say what one sees
> To share one's love to sing to search for
>   rhymes
> I really do not know what they want of me
>   Is it really really a crime
>
> To dream of happiness in the jaws of the wolf
> And to say at midnight that the lark is near
> My friends my friends and it is from you however
> That comes the reproach
>
> Landscape Go on I know what they are saying
> *One must paint history one must paint struggle*
> And why do you come at the height of the tragedy
> To play a melody on a flute for us[32]

To all reproaches, Aragon replies that he is not seeking safety, nor is he
practicing that evasion he has condemned since his earliest works. He has
never closed his eyes to the suffering of mankind and has always been
found in the front ranks in moments of danger. Did anyone sing more
loudly than he at the time of France's greatest peril? No, he replies, this is
not evasion:

> I claim the right to dream at the turning
> Of the road Of the great charms of the walk
> The right to be moved by the world now
> That the cannonade is approaching
> . . . .
> I claim the right to believe in the future

> To believe in music in happiness in nature
> In the great sun that makes golden leaves
> dance for us
> On the trees of the road[33]

There are constant references to old age and death throughout *Les Yeux et la mémoire*:

> And I thought that on a similar day not very
> far off
> I will no more come back to you with beating
> heart
> . . . .
> I will no longer touch your hair in the evening
> I will no longer suffer at never seeing you
>
> I will no longer feel my heart beat
> At the sound of your voice in the next room[34]

Despite this realization, the basic note of *Les Yeux et la mémoire* is optimistic:

> There is one thing that I cannot understand
> It is this fear of dying people have
> As if it were not sufficiently marvelous
> That for a moment the sky seemed tender to us
> Despite war and injustice and insomnia
> When one carries this fox of bitterness
> Eating out one's heart and God knows that I have
> Carried it like a clinging child all my life
> . . . .
> Despite everything I tell you that this life was
> such
> That to those who wish to listen to me to those
> whom I address here
> No longer having on my lips but the single word
> thanks
> I say despite everything that this life was
> beautiful[35]

The thought of his death and imminent separation from Elsa does not elicit from Aragon an egotistical response. He does not regret that the world will continue without him but, on the contrary, seeks to contribute to a universal future of happiness, one in which a love like his and Elsa's will be the rule, rather than the exception.

V   Le Roman inachevé

This work, which was published two years after *Les Yeux et la mémoire*, is not a novel as the title would suggest. The word *roman* here is used in its medieval sense, denoting a true or imaginary narrative in prose or in verse written in the vulgar tongue. Thus, the French title can perhaps be best translated as *The Unfinished Romance*. Here Aragon takes up again the themes of the previous poem, but the work is more subjective and introspective and less aggressively political. In verses reminiscent of his first poems in *Feu de joie*, he tells of the days when: "You suddenly feel in your arms the dimensions of the world/And your own strength and that everything is suddenly possible."[36] But childhood ended on the "atrocious doorstep" of war and nothing remained of the wonders of youth. After the war, continues Aragon, "words took me by the hand," and he describes the Surrealist adventure:

> Here begins the great night of words
> Here the name is separated from what it
> designates
> . . . .
> It begins this way words lead you
> You lose sight of roofs you lose sight of
> land You follow
> Inexplicably the path of the birds[37]

But all that was a dream, nothing he recounted really happened, wrote Aragon, before the miracle of love:

> A love that is born is the wonderland on the
> other side of the mirror
> A woman is a door that opens on the unknown
> . . . .
> One leaves everything for a woman and everything
> takes on another dimension
> Everything harmonizes with her voice Woman
> is the Marvelous
> Everything becomes transfigured at her passage[38]

Again, he intones the litany: "My life really began/The day I met you,"

> And life went by like a flash of lightning
> streaking the sky
> I listen in the depths of myself to the fading
> sound of my own steps
> . . . .

> It seems that there has been nothing but my
> love in my life
> I have never done anything except through you
> for the love of you[39]

But life, even one devoted to love, is like "running water between our hands."[40] Each day he becomes more aware of his age:

> I will never again hold in my arms
> The sea which flung itself and rolled me
> in foam
> Until we both finally became tired
>
> For a long time now I have lost the habit
> Of challenging the snow and climbing the
> peaks
> In the dazzle of the sun and fog[41]

Why, then, he asks, do I persist in living? And the answer is that he lives for Elsa. Her presence brings him an eternal rejuvenation and appeases his bitterness:

> Wherever you go I follow you Life is in
> your wake
> I hold you to me Everything else is a mirage
> . . . .
> No I never suffer when I hold you in my arms
> It is through you that I live Elsa of my youth
> What would I be without you but a man adrift[42]

It was Elsa who taught him happiness, the happiness of loving and of being loved, and it is because of this love that he can face with equanimity the horror of aging and the miseries of life.

VI Elsa

This long work, published in 1959, again recounts the story of the love of Louis Aragon and Elsa Triolet from their first meeting at the Coupole until the moment when the last line of the poem was written. The poet speaks not only subjectively of his great love, but also of a woman in relationship to her profession and to society. He employs verses of varying meters, including the classical alexandrine. However, the preferred form in the work is free verse, the long sweeping lines that Aragon called "uncounted" verses in his earlier treatises on versification.

This work was influenced by *Roses à crédit*, a novel in Elsa's series of novels "L'Âge de Nylon." On the flyleaf of his work, Aragon quotes the lines from Elsa's novel that particularly inspired his poem: "It was in 1958 that there appeared on the market the perfumed rose 'Martine Donelle:' it has the unsurpassable odor of the ancient rose, and the color and shape of the modern rose." Elsa's novel explains Aragon's use of the rose as a symbol throughout his poem:

> You who are the rose oh mysterious rose
> at this time of the year
> . . . .
> When everything is but praise of your
> glory and of your likeness
> Oh rose that is your being and your name
> . . . .
> *I will invent the rose for you*[43]

He speaks of the "paradox of December," a love that has grown even greater since tne springtime of their lives: "Oh beauty that is ending oh beauty even more beautiful at the end/Oh my love as beautiful as the end of the year/Oh rose of the end of the year."[44]

In verses reminiscent of the poetry of the sixteenth century, he sings of his love, comparing her beauty to that of the rose, and also of the timeless themes of dawn, of awakening, of love, and fear of death. I know now why I was born, he writes:

> Before me is the great truth of the winter
> Every man has the destiny of a spark Every man
> Is ephemeral and in what way am I more than
> any man
> My pride is that I loved
>
> Nothing else
>
> And the stone plunges endlessly into the
> dust of the planets
> I am but a bit of spilled wine but the wine
> Bears witness to drunkenness in the wan light
> of dawn
>
> Nothing else
>
> I was born for these words I have spoken
>
> My love[45]

The love of which he sings is a fusion of both body and soul: "When you sleep in my arms I can slowly caress your soul."[46] He sings a hymn of praise to Elsa who fashioned his blind, unheeding soul to her likeness and taught him that he was a human being. Open my books anywhere, he writes, a single refrain is all that you will find, a long hymn of praise,

> The endless Ave of the litanies
> My perpetual insomnia
> My blooming my adornment
> Oh my reason oh my madness
> My month of May my melody
> My paradise my fire
>
> My universe Elsa my life[47]

His adoration for Elsa has become a religion, he is the "heretic of all churches,"[48] his love for her goes beyond any human or divine love. The love of Elsa is carried to the point of idolatry, and it is for this idolatry of a woman that the madman in *Le Fou d'Elsa* (1963) is tried and convicted by his judges.

With his love, Aragon offers to Elsa the gift of his jealousy. The theme of jealousy runs throughout Aragon's work. In the early "Amour d'Elsa," written in a *précieux* vein, the poet expresses his jealousy of everything and anything that enters into the life of Elsa, from the drops of rain that "seem too much like kisses" when they fall upon her, to her memories, her thoughts, and her silences. In *Elsa*, he reveals his initial jealousy of her creativity, of her life apart from his. He writes that no one will ever understand the torture and the jealousy he experienced when Elsa first was cruel enough to show him those "children" she had by herself. No one will understand his overwhelming curiosity about her dreams, nor the anguish he felt one day when, in order to create one of her works, she imagined that he was dead. Each time that he looks at her now, he remembers that she imagined the world without him.[49]

In "La Chambre d'Elsa," a prose play in one act that appears in *Elsa*, Aragon describes himself as he is seated in Elsa's room, an old man with eyes only for her, "a past that still survives itself by a few minutes."[50] When he looks at her, it is clear that he is excluded from her thoughts. But now he is accustomed to this and he no longer protests against it. Indeed, he no longer suffers jealousy because he has become resigned to the knowledge that a man cannot possess the mind of a woman.

The last poem of *Elsa* expresses once again the essence of all of Aragon's love poetry:

One day Elsa my verses will be your crown
And will survive me because they are worn by you
They will be understood better in their
    diversity
Through this reflection of you given to them
    by your hair
One day Elsa my verses because of your eyes
Of your penetrating soft eyes which were able
    to see
As no one else could tomorrow in the last light
    of evening
One day Elsa they will understand my verses

Then they will understand, concludes Aragon, "that my night prepared the morning."[51]

VII   Les Poètes

Les Poètes (1960), which follows *Le Roman inachevé* and *Elsa*, is a collection of poems in which are found themes of love and friendship intermingled with an essay on poetics. Aragon pays homage to the poets of the past and seeks to provide insight into the phenomenon of poetry and the nature of the poet:

A poet is one who writes poems
A poem is the form that poetry takes
But what is what is poetry

This thing in me this thing outside of me[52]

He defines poetry as the carrying of knowledge beyond its mere acquisition, and the poet as the one who goes beyond direct experience to create an image from a hypothesis. Taking reality as his point of departure, he perceives a relationship that has never before been noticed. It is almost as if the poet were endowed with an unknown sixth sense, which Aragon calls "poetic radar." It is not only the poet's life that is transformed by his poetry, but also the lives of those who heed his message. In keeping with the Romantic ideal of the poet as guide and leader of mankind, Aragon compares the poet to Prometheus. He uses the ancient myth to symbolize the process of artistic creation.

I pay less for having given fire to mankind
Than for this hope in their eyes and life in
    their arms
Like a woman

> Tomorrow like a child
> I pay for having given man the certainty
> That he makes the world in his own image
> . . . .
> I pay for what man does without limit[53]

The poet pays for having given man the certainty that he is master of his own destiny.

Aragon writes, in *Les Poètes*, that there is a new world to conquer and that poetry must occupy its rightful place in it. Often, he interrupts the poem to write in prose just as history at times took his elbow and forced him to write as it dictated. Then, he felt an irresistible pressure to "say things simply make that suffering within you sing for others simply speak to them the language that cuts their bread speak directly to them like one who is asking for a room in the inn . . ."[54]

The verses of *Les Poètes* are those of an old man preoccupied with death:

> Childhood was only yesterday and I had no
>   sooner put on the velvet gloves of my
>   springtime
> Then I became a toothless rag already incapable
>   of climbing mountains
>
> I have arrived without even noticing it at
>   this very point of death
> At this point from which you can only look
>   back because there is nothing further
>   before you[55]

The sadness of old age makes even more unbearable the misery of the world:

> The world is badly constituted my heart is
>   weary
> For lack of courage or audacity
> Everything goes along as usual nothing has
>   changed
> One comes to terms with danger
> Age comes without anything having happened[56]

However much he may be troubled by the misery of the world, he continues, "never will I lose that wonder over language":

> The heaven of words within me its vague
>   scintillation
> This starry multitude within me
> I have not ceased to be wonder struck at words at
>   this night
> Of words in me Of that dust in me of a long
>   Sunday
> That light divided to infinity and who
>   will explain to me
> The strange joining of their kaleidoscopes
> The collisions of colors the architecture
>   of the song
>
> Internal cosmos as beautiful as joined hands
> I have not finished I will never cease to wonder at
> These formations of crystal these precipitations
>   of words[57]

He is reconciled to his own death, provided that his words live on after him to bear witness to what he was.

And then, "Elsa enters into the poem," and the poet sings to her:

> Music of my life oh my perfume my wife
> Take possession of me to the depths of the
>   soul
>
> Enter into my poem my sole passion
> Let it be solely your breath
>
> Immobile without you deserted by your absence
> Let it finally take meaning and power from you [58]

The words "I love you" are the sum of all Aragon has learned in this world. For him, these words are "the punctuation of the drama of life."[59]

VIII Il ne m'est Paris que d'Elsa. Le Voyage de Hollande

In 1964, two collections of poems appeared in the series devoted to Elsa. In both of these works, it is the poet's wife who gives meaning and beauty to the landscape. *Il ne m'est Paris que d'Elsa* is both a subjective and objective guide to Paris in which the verses are accompanied by photographs of the city. Verses from the poems serve as captions for the pictures.

"Once upon a time there was a meaningless Paris," begins the now familiar story. Then, Elsa entered the café in Montparnasse that fateful evening in 1928. "I love nothing except through you and Paris to me is only Elsa," the poet continues.[60] He describes the twenty-five years he has spent with Elsa in Paris: "I have watched you sleep for a quarter of a century in the Vendôme quarter. . . . For a quarter of a century listening to my love beat within me like a metronome."[61] But time passes inexorably, and before lovers have a chance to love, their hair is gray. Now that the poet is old, Paris is no longer his city, it belongs to the young. It is only a reflection of the past and a mirage of the future. Then, in a song which praises the perfection of shared love, Aragon offers to Elsa "this bouquet of Paris of the future."[62]

In the second part of this collection are reprinted some of Aragon's most famous poems celebrating his love for Paris, his suffering during his exile from the city, and his joyful return. Included are poems devoted to heroes and artists whose names are inseparable from the name of their city. Among these is "Mme Colette," the novelist of Paris, awaiting death as she watches her beloved city through her windows:

> Youth my youth is it then your reflection
> One survives for a long time the April of
> kisses
> Noon is astonished already and looks for the
> dew
> Even a beautiful dusk still causes pain
> The heart that remembers is never appeased[63]

Death is ever present here as Aragon describes in the concluding section his feelings toward death:

> It takes time to truly imagine this universe
> without one
> One's eternal absence from the deep heart of
> mirrors
> . . . .
> It takes time to unweave this link between
> oneself and the world[64]

But, if nothing remains of me after I die, he concludes, at least I know today that the future will remember that in these troubled times there was in this world someone who placed love above all.

The poems of *Le Voyage de Hollande* were inspired by a trip to the Netherlands. They sing of the joys of love and of the discovery of a country through this love. But, wherever Aragon may go, he tells his beloved,

> There is nothing to see but your face
> Nothing to hear but your beloved voice
> For whether or not my eyes are closed
> I have only you for a landscape
>
> . . . .
>
> Breughel of Hell or of Velvet
> Windmills tulips devilry
> Holland in my reveries
> Is only my love only my love[65]

The collection closes with a mass, "La Messe d'Elsa," which includes an introit, an orison, a credo, an offertory, and an elevation. This mass offered to Elsa carries out the intention expressed in Aragon's work since *La Peinture au défi*, to redirect Christian mysticism and to substitute a human liturgy capable of singing of Elsa and the future. The poet has created a new mythology organized around Elsa and his relationship with her. It is because Elsa represents love, hope, and the future that he dedicates to her a poetic cult which, in *Le Fou d'Elsa*, becomes a religion.

IX Le Fou d'Elsa

In *Le Fou d'Elsa* (*Elsa's Madman*), published in 1963, we find the highest expression of the poet's adoration of Elsa. It is a monumental epic in six parts with an epilogue and includes about two hundred selections in prose and in poetry. These are followed by a historical, philological, and philosophical lexicon. The work is both a historical meditation on the destiny of the last Moorish king of Andalusia before the fall of Granada to the Spanish in 1492, and an impassioned quest for the meaning of man, the tragedy of man and the future of mankind.

The preface and the preliminary canto describe the circumstances which inspired this work. Everything began as a result of an error in an old song "The Eve of the Fall of Granada," in which the first verse, "La veille où Grenade fut prise," contained an ellipsis of the words "the fall." It was this omission that set Aragon to dreaming about the Moslem Granada that had figured in his childhood texts. The words "the fall of Granada" also brought forth for Aragon memories of the terrible June 13 when he heard that Paris had fallen to the Germans, as well as memories of the poet Federico Garcia-Lorca whose blood was spilled in Granada. Elsa, too, translated for him the poem of Mikhail Svetlow, "Granada my love Granada Granada," on which she had based her novel of 1956, *Le Rendez-vous des étrangers*. It was perhaps her book that finally stimulated Aragon to express all the emotions for Granada that had lain dormant within him.

The Love of Elsa and the Great Poetic Works

Why do we create legendary countries for ourselves if they are to become places of exile for our hearts? Everything that ever intoxicated me, everything that ever turned my head, whether music, painting, heroism, poetry, when I look back, I seem to see it flow towards me from all sides, converge in me as if to sow a single piece of land, to prepare the harvest of my life, prepare the compost for my love. Wagner, Tchaikovsky, Shakespeare or Rimbaud ... a man is only an instrument made ready for the hands of a woman which model him and refashion him from the brute he was.... It is not coincidence, but convergence. The day had to come, on which I received from the woman I loved exclusively, I mean the only woman I will have loved, a song from her far off country, strangely obsessed with Granada. [66]

Perhaps it was because of this book, continued Aragon, that he felt the necessity of writing a work in which he could express so many things that were within him. "What was Granada to me before Elsa but a vague yearning like any other? Every seed needs both the soil and the sun to flower. And it is thus that Granada rose from the land of my dreams to the light of the woman who had pronounced its name ..."[67]

The first part of *Le Fou d'Elsa* introduces the reader to Moorish Granada and to its last king, Boabdil. Spanish history and legend have given a biased portrait of this king, whose true nature Aragon attempts to uncover in this poem. Rejecting the accusations against Boabdil made by those who recorded the chronicles of the Spanish Reconquest, Aragon went in search of the true Boabdil "throughout the entire forest of Islam.... And it was not only about that Child-King that I had to refashion my ideas. I belonged by tradition, education and prejudices to the Christian world: that is why I could not have access to the world of Islam by the direct route of study or travel. Here I could only be guided by dreams (and intuition), like those who descended into Hell, Orpheus or Dante."[68]

It is in the market, L'Alcaiceria, that first appears Kéis l'Amirite, the Andalusian troubadour, the Madman, who sings about his beloved Elsa. This mad troubadour is patterned on the "Medjnoûn Leilâ," a hero of Arab tradition who reputedly lived in the first century of the Hegira. Kéis had fallen in love with the beautiful Leilâ who returned his love, but her father refused his suit. Mad with grief, Kéis wandered about the world composing verses about his passion, thereby acquiring the sobriquet "Leilâ's Madman." The theme was used by many authors over the centuries, but the most beautiful version is that of the Persian poet Djâmî, who composed his *Medjnoûn et Leilâ* eight years before the fall of Granada. Aragon's hero has identified himself with Leilâ's lover so completely that, like him, he has lost his own name to be known henceforth as the Madman, substituting only the name of his beloved, Elsa, for the name of Leilâ. While continuing the lyrical tradition of the Medjnoûn Leilâ, Aragon's hero, like an idolator, worships a woman foreign to Islam. He incurs the hatred and scorn of those around him with his love, which violates all accepted rules of love and which seems a reproach to all those who live tranquilly with their wives and concubines. Despite their persecution, continues the poet, "I who am going to die, who must use each breath sparingly in order to name Elsa . . . give you here the poems of the Medjnoûn . . . who speaks for me in the Granada called life, where I fear neither shame nor laughter, but only that I will not have said before nightfall what I was born to say."[69]

The next section is composed of the songs of the Medjnoûn which have been gathered together by his servant boy Zaid. The boy has saved only his love poems because "writing is not made for transitory things, but for things that endure . . . the future of man is woman and not kings."[70] Zaid's commentaries after each poem explain their allegorical meaning and their relationship to the lives of Aragon and Elsa. He explains that the only perfect rhyme is man and woman. All poetry is the art of living by twos, and a day will come, he believes, when the perfection called "couple" will be triumphant throughout the world.[71] Love poems in every meter and of every type are included in this section. The richly rhymed "Vers à danser" in eight syllables, has already been set to music:

> Whether it be Sunday or Monday
> Night or morning midnight noon
> In hell or in paradise
> Loves all resemble one another
> It was yesterday that I said to you
> We will sleep together
>
> . . . .
> My love what was will be
> Heaven stretches over us like a sheet
> I have closed my arms around you
> And I love you so much that I tremble
> As long as you wish
> We will sleep together[72]

The second chapter of *Le Fou d'Elsa* tells of the civil strife in Granada before the Christian conquest and recounts the battles with the Christians. Particular emphasis is placed on the Battle of Rondah in which cannon were used for the first time and which represented the start of "eternal terror." Chapter III, entitled "1490," shows Boabdil reigning at the Alhambra. He knows from an ancient prediction that he will be the last Moorish king in Spain. Heir to the misfortunes of his country, he symbolizes not only the tragedy of a king, but also the tragedy of mankind. "Each misery is a kingdom in which one of us is king."[73] Then the

Medjnoûn intervenes to sing a *zadjal*, a poem of the future. This is one of the most significant poems in the book, since it proclaims the essential message of the poet:

> The future of man is woman
> She is the color of his soul
> She is his sound and his echo
> And without her he is but a blasphemy
> He is only a stone without the fruit
> . . . .\. . . . .
> I tell you that man is born for
> Woman and born for love
> Everything of the old world is going to change
> First life and then death
> And all things shared
> The white bread the kisses that bleed
> One will see the reign of the couple
> Snow down like orange blossoms[74]

Chapter IV, "1491," is composed of a series of poems on the relationship between man and time, another important theme in the work of Aragon. The Medjnoûn is arraigned for heresy because he has been discovered praying to a woman instead of to God. The Câdi, the supreme judge of Granada, sends his men in search of the woman to whom he addressed his prayers, but they are unable to find her. The Medjnoûn tells them that they cannot find her, nor can he send for her, because she exists four and one-half centuries ahead in the future. The Câdi asks how he can say that this woman does and does not exist. He replies that she does not exist according to the Câdi's vision of the world. She exists, he insists, because she is going to exist. The Medjnoûn is beaten and placed in a cave of prisoners because of his heresy. His jailers beat him and force him to sing and, from his torn and broken mouth, comes forth a song of love that resembles the song Solomon sang to his Queen of Sheba.

Chapter V, "La Veille où Grenade fut prise," tells of the last hours before the fall of the kingdom. The Medjnoûn takes refuge in a cave of gypsies and, from this cave, he sees visions of the future. He sees how the triumph of Catholicism will place obstacles in the way of the realization of the couple for centuries to come. The principal figures of Spanish literature pass before his eyes. All of them, from La Celestina of Fernando de Rojas to Don Juan, show how the concept of courtly love was degraded throughout the centuries. Don Juan, whose concept of love was limited to seduction because he regarded woman as an object, represents the negation of love and of the couple. In Catholic Spain, the language of love was altered to become the language of mystic love, the most magnificent exponents of which were Sainte Thérèse d'Avila and Saint Jean de la Croix: "Jean de la Croix you are but the Christian name of all those who love to the point of madness/ . . . In this world love is the fulfillment of man Jean de la Croix."[75] The Medjnoûn then looks beyond the seducer and the saint for a sign of a couple and believes that he sees this couple at the beginning of the nineteenth century in François René de Chateaubriand and his beloved Nathalie de Noailles. He is present at their secret meeting in the gardens of the Alhambra, but they are incapable of achieving perfect communion because "the time of the couple still has not come."[76]

Then the Medjnoûn approaches Elsa's time and is seized with anguish because nothing has changed, because lasting love is still a chimera. Men have found scientific discoveries more important than the establishment of the couple. Ribbi Abraham, a learned doctor who has also taken refuge in the cave, explains that the sickness of the Medjnoûn stems from the coexistence within him of both normal time and accelerated time. Parallel to his real life, he has led an imaginary existence of variable rhythm which permitted him to traverse centuries in a few months. Now that he has reached the twentieth century, he has reached an equilibrium, both times have become of equal length. The poet is one who, like the Medjnoûn, lives a double life because he carries within himself both normal time of limited horizons and an accelerated time, a tragic inner haste which stems from the knowledge that the duration of time changes as the time left to one grows shorter. Because he understands, the poet is able to explain the relationship between human time and historical time. The future is the reconciliation of these two movements of time. It was in order to see this future that Aragon was compelled to reinvent the past:

> I threw myself back into the time before my
>   life
> I went back four centuries before my birth
> And I sought from that lost Granada to the
>   century of Elsa the law of progress
>   the mechanism
> By which man goes beyond man and each
>   generation
> Becomes a higher rung on the ladder
> . . . .
> I reinvented the past to see the beauty
>   of the future[77]

The Medjnoûn expresses the poet's dream of a future of man and woman together, each being for the other the answer to all questions, whom nothing can separate and from whom will stem the beauty of the world. The first and last experiences of the human being are, in reality, the adventure of love. The Medjnoûn, an old man who is the same age as Aragon, sings of the future he perceives:

> This life is ending
> Love my only absolute
> For you suns are rising
> Which no longer have dusks[78]

CHAPTER 6

Toward a New Novel

I La Mise à mort

"I believe that the twentieth century will be not only the century of the atomic bomb, but also the century in which the novel will no longer be the work of a few men who are satisfied to develop it linearly, but a sort of gigantic collective enterprise, comparable to science," wrote Aragon in *J'Abats mon jeu,*[1] and it is to the task of creating this new novel that Aragon has devoted himself in his vast novels *La Mise à mort* (1965) and *Blanche ou l'oubli* (1967). It is Aragon's contention that novels are dreams that the author shares with his readers. A novel is dated not by the dream expressed, but by the form used by the dreamer-novelist to set down his dream. While the form may vary in our changing world, taking on what Aragon calls the color of its age, there remains constantly alive the treasury of stories in which neither Oedipus, nor Tristan, nor Hamlet dies, but is reborn eternally, to reappear on the stage with new props, new actors, and in a changed perspective.

The title of *La Mise à mort* (*The Moment of Truth*) is taken from a poem by Boris Pasternak, which was translated into French by Elsa:

> Old age is Rome which
> Instead of chariots and stadiums
> Demands not comedy
> But that the death blow be dealt[2]

This long work is that of the old man who, in *Les Yeux et la mémoire*, demanded for himself the right to dream at the turning of the road. Writing against the clock, in this "conversation by means of the novel which is the very language of love, of the reality called love,"[3] he expresses again his great passion. Taking as his point of departure the verses of John Donne: "I wonder by my troth, what thou and I Did, till we lov'd," Aragon writes:

And one day, suddenly, you remember . . . you appeared on my accursed path, it was November and I no longer wanted to die . . . you were what one could ask of no one, I had to take you, and taking you was still meaningless, because afterwards it was necessary to win you. I became that thief who no longer lived except for the stolen object, and I know very well that one day it will be necessary to pay the price for every moment.... You became for me, love, the image of the world which I will never be permitted to enter, you became for me, love, the unattainable summertime of man.[4]

La Mise à mort is a long work which contains, in addition to an impassioned poetic song of love and jealousy, a wealth of personal reflections, historical episodes, and contemporary events. Within the novel, there are also three separate novelettes which were originally written for a collection of short stories. The basic problem dealt with in this work is the Pirandellian theme of the plurality of the human personality, the split existing in the "double men" about whom Aragon wrote in "Le Monde réel." In *Les Beaux Quartiers*, Aragon described the duality present in all of the actions and thoughts of Joseph Quesnel. Two contradictory concepts of the world coexisted within this man; he was two antagonistic, inseparable individuals.

This duality is presented in *La Mise à mort* in such a way that the reader believes at first that he is reading about two men, Anthoine and Alfred, and two women, the famous singer Ingeborg d'Usher and Anthoine's mistress Fougère, who is also the passion of Alfred's life. Only later does the reader realize that Fougère is Alfred's private name for Ingeborg d'Usher and that Anthoine is Fougère's private image of Alfred. The names of Aragon and Elsa appear from time to time in the midst of this mythical quartet, but it is the interchanges between Anthoine, Alfred, Ingeborg, and Fougère that make up the plot of the novel. The duality of the human personality leads in *La Mise à mort* to a discourse on the ambivalence of Dr. Jekyll and Mr. Hyde, Stevenson's creation that has become part of the eternal treasury of the novel. Stevenson started his novel by stating: "I want to tell you about a fellow who was two fellows." However, writes Aragon, Stevenson's hero was only the first step; the split between the philanthropist and the monster presupposes a rather elementary view of the many facets of the human personality. Joseph Quesnel of "Le Monde réel" represented a step forward from Stevenson's hero, since his double nature did not require the childish device of the physical division into two vastly divergent appearances. The physical appearance of Dr. Jekyll was so different from that of Mr. Hyde that they were unrecognizable as the same person. With Quesnel, the division existed in ideas alone, so that he was able, in all good conscience, to perform actions in his public role that he condemned privately.

When Stevenson wrote the story of Dr. Jekyll and Mr. Hyde in 1885, he was able to do so only within the frame of reference available to him. He was incapable of imagining the decomposition of the personality without the introduction of an external stimulus such as the magic potion consumed by his hero. Nor could he imagine that good and evil might coexist and that the appearance of Mr. Hyde did not necessarily call for the disappearance of Dr. Jekyll. Such coexistence, states Aragon, requires the presence of a third man, a mediator between the two, and it is this third inner incarnation of man, "the Indifferent," whom Aragon introduces in *La Mise à mort* under the name of Christian Fustel-Schmidt. The "human trinity" is symbolized by a three-way mirror in which Christian sees reflected the three components of his personality.

The theme of the mirror has recurred throughout Aragon's work. In his early Surrealist texts, the mirror provided a passageway into another world. The Surrealist Jean Cocteau used the mirror in similar fashion in his play *Orpheus*. When Orpheus discovers that Eurydice has been stolen away by Death, he decides to pursue her. The Angel Heurtebise gives him a pair of magic gloves which enables him to pass through the mirror to the world hidden beyond the world of appearances. He tells Orpheus that mirrors are doors through which Death comes and goes and that, whenever he looks into the mirror, he will see death reflected there. In a chapter of *La Mise à mort*, entitled "Digression on the Novel as a Mirror," Aragon returns to this Surrealist theme of mirrors as a means of access to new realities. He cites as an authority on this subject Lewis Carroll's Alice. Since he first translated Carroll's *The Hunting of the Snark* in 1928, Aragon has been fascinated by all of Carroll's work, particularly by the first chapter of *Through the Looking Glass*. "Oh, Kitty! " Alice says to her cat, "how nice it would be if we could only get through into Looking-glass house! ... Let's pretend that there's a way of getting through it, some-how Kitty."[5] It is this "let's pretend," states Aragon, that constitutes all the art of the novel, and it is with this "let's pretend" that he begins each chapter of his novel. "But, as for me, if I am no longer young enough to make conversation with little cats, there still remains the question of crossing the mirror, of passing into the house on the other side, that is to say, of entering into the world on the other side that is forbidden to me, this world that is you."[6]

The mirror hides the profound inner life even of the beloved and thus symbolizes the distance between two people. In *Elsa*, when Aragon described Elsa seated at her dressing table, looking into her mirror, he remarked: "It is not certain that she sees herself there, it is perhaps a stratagem to leave the room, to reach areas that are forbidden to the man, which escape his commentaries."[7] In *La Mise à mort*, he becomes aware when he watches his beloved sleep that he can only see the woman as she reflects his idea of her. He can never pass beyond the wall of appearances into the world of her dreams. He can never cross the mirror which is the screen placed between him and what transpires within her. So desperately does he want to persuade her to reveal her dreams, that he opens up the secret world of his dreams to her. That is what he calls writing, and he writes for no other reason than to permit her to see beyond the mirror. Everything is secondary to his effort to penetrate her secret thoughts: "But after all, let everything that we were perish if, during this little dream of the two of us, I have been able to hear this song and break this magic wall which separates us."[8]

While the mirror is used by Aragon to symbolize the barrier between individuals, it also serves for him as the link between the individual and the rest of humanity. It is in the mirror that he sees reflected, alongside of his own image, what he has called "the others." In one of the most celebrated poems of *La Diane française*, "Elsa at the Mirror," Elsa sees reflected in her mirror the deaths of their companions in the Resistance:

> It was in the midst of our tragedy
> And all day long sitting at her mirror
> She combed her golden hair I seemed to see
> Her patient hands quiet a blaze
> It was in the midst of our tragedy
> . . . .
> And all day long seated at her mirror
> She saw reflected there dying in the distance
>
> One by one the actors of our tragedy
> The best in this accursed world[9]

The mirror also bears witness to the inexorable passage of time. Not only does the three-way mirror reflect the "human trinity," it also reflects the three components of time, the present in the center which carries along with it the side images of the past and future "as if all present were but the past of a future, as if all past were but a symbol of things to come."[10]

The obsession with the mirror can become the lover's obsession at being nothing more than the reflection of his beloved. "Imagine. . . . This mirror in which you do not see yourself but only her. Imagine the mirror-time inhabited by the image-love."[11] In *La Mise à mort*, Anthoine has lost the ability to see his own image in the mirror, since he owes his existence entirely to the image Fougère has of him. It was one night when Fougère was singing that he lost his image. Until then, he had been like the rest of the world, judging everything egotistically, solely in its relationship to himself. His reflection then corresponded perfectly to the idea he had of himself. But, one evening when Fougère sang, he lost this subjectivity and began to see the world objectively. It was Fougère's voice that taught him about the existence of others, and from this knowledge emerged another image of himself. From that moment on, he became a realist:

When she sings, I love her soul bestially. It goes beyond all understanding. Sometimes the melody reaches a paroxysm of ecstasy that makes me pale, without my having to verify it in the mirror.... What am I saying? These are mad things. But loving is nothing other than taking leave of one's senses, isn't it? What is most extraordinary about Fougère is that, however beautiful the music may be, she still makes the words reach you. The height of knowledge is when the sentence achieves the grandeur of banality, when what is said is so simple that one is absolutely disconcerted by it.[12]

La Mise à mort is also a book about jealousy, for he who is not jealous cannot be in love. Fougère's song makes Anthoine jealous, not of someone, but of what he is not. For his study of jealousy, Aragon again returns to the treasury of literature and includes a digression on Othello, who is transformed into a murderer by jealousy. Aragon believes that jealousy is linked to the highest expression of love, because it manifests itself as a result of the impossibility of total communion with the beloved, and the impossibility of absolute love. The jealous person is not the ridiculous figure who appears so frequently in literature, but an individual who is rendered tragic by his solitude and his passion. There is nothing more elevated, more noble in man than this jealousy: "I say that man is only a man if he achieves this zenith of humanity which is to be constantly and totally jealous of each breath and each pause between breaths."[13] The jealousy of the lover extends both to the past and to the future, for in the happiness of love is concealed a mortal fear. "My life and my novel are you and I am abominably jealous of death."[14]

Alfred is jealous of Anthoine who is the image Fougère has of him. Anthoine's militant political life separates him from the apolitical Alfred. "Torn as I was between being what I was and what Anthoine was believed to be, I began to consider it my duty to make an exemplary character out of him ... Anthoine was my atonement."[15] Alfred finally decides to kill Anthoine. His madness comes not from his plurality, but from the fact that being both one and multiple, he has, in a schizophrenic frenzy, destroyed all unity by a sharp division into his multiple selves. From the point of view of contemporary realism, he knows that killing Anthoine is going to deprive him of his positive hero and that, without this positive hero, he will appear somewhat frivolous, but, in a fit of madness, he smashes the reflection of Anthoine which he finally sees in the mirror. Fougère discovers him lying on the ground, an old man with white hair, directly in front of the broken mirror. When she anxiously questions the doctor about the extent of his injuries, the doctor replies that she must be courageous. "He will live of course, but . . . how can I say it? . . . he loved you, Madame, you must understand, he loved you *to the point of madness*."[16]

Aragon's theory of the novel is similar to that of Norman Mailer, who sees the novel as a great instrument of collective knowledge, a means for social vision. Thus it is that Aragon's mirror reflects the bitterness of a world made more bitter by the revelations of Stalin's atrocities. When the novelist looks into the mirror, he sees "this empty world, like a room hastily abandoned, the book thrown on the ground, torn, torn."[17] He tells of how his friend Michael Koltsov, a Communist journalist, was executed under Stalin, and cries: "How bitter, bitter is everything, I think of you Michel, of what the future would have been like with those who dreamed of living according to the laws of justice. . . . What disorder, my God, what disorder. It is not only I who have lost my image. An entire century can no longer compare its soul with what it sees. And we may be counted in the millions, we who are the lost children of this immense divorce."[18]

Anicet had dreamed of systematizing life, the Peasant of Paris had dreamed of a new order, the Communist believed that changing the methods of distribution would bring about this new order and that Socialist Realism would both reflect this order and contribute to it. But the promises proved illusory, and Aragon expresses for the first time a hostile attitude toward Socialist Realism. Socialist Realism puts the cart before the horse, states Aragon, since it places upon the artist the burden of changing the world. In order to make the rules of Socialist Realism worth-while, it is necessary to change not the brain of the novelist, but the world. The writers might in all fairness reproach the politicians for not having produced the positive heroes they need as models for their novels, instead of being reproached by them for not furnishing the people with heroes to emulate. Aragon's final gesture of defiance is to kill his positive hero, Anthoine. The creator of Joseph Gigoux, the blind, optimistic hero of *Les Communistes*, destroys what this man symbolized when he kills Anthoine. Just before Alfred commits this murder, he utters a terrible cry of anguish at the ultimate loneliness of love and of man:

Never will you know what stifles me. . . . Because everything seems precisely as if what I betray to you is my secret, doesn't it? While the truth lies elsewhere. This banal fiction I drag out. This despair. This despair of an entire life. These silent sobs, these dry tears. This abomination of existing. And I turn around to see what is following me, this shadow. As far back as my memory goes, this silent sea . . . nothing of that abyss within me sings, and I hear in the distance only the convulsion before the cry, I hear only that rising within me, that accumulation of the unbearable, that growth that fills me, that black ripening that comes from the depths of existence, always brushed aside in vain only to return, and I am there, I pretend, I smile at times with that mouth, bitter for me alone, with which I recount, I recount . . . there is no one . . . who can know, guess, share this trembling of my soul, this lassitude in the depths of my flesh, no one, I am alone, stop pretending.[19]

II Blanche ou l'oubli (Blanche or Forgetfulness)

Aragon has described *Blanche ou l'oubli* (1967) as a book on the novel, which in turn becomes a theory of the novel. It centers about the desperate efforts of the protagonist Geoffroy Gaiffier to overcome his forgetfulness and to recapture, through his writing, his wife Blanche. It is by means of the novel he is writing and other novels he has read that Gaiffier attempts to understand his life and to discover why his wife left him after twenty years together: ". . . I try by means of the novel to make sure of what I am, of what I could have been, I try by this strange method to find you in my arms again, as if you had never escaped from them."[20] Aragon's thesis is that the novel is not a source of amusement or escape, but rather a means for acquiring knowledge. The great novels one has read are as much a part of one's background and heritage as anything else that might occur within one's life. Each novel produces a certain change within the reader. Throughout *Blanche ou l'oubli*, Gaiffier describes the way in which his reading has affected him. He states that Johann-Christian Friedrich Holderlin entered his life in 1922, the year in which he first read his novel *Hyperion*. Flaubert's *Education sentimentale* affected him so, that it is impossible for him to stop at the corner of the rue Tronchet and the rue Vignon without experiencing the bitterness felt by the hero of that novel as he waited vainly for his beloved Mme Arnoux on the day of the uprising of February, 1848. Whenever he sees a man hesitate to cross the rue Vignon, he thinks this man must be thinking about Mme Arnoux. *L'Education sentimentale* and Flaubert, *Hyperion* and Holderlin, as well as Elsa Triolet and her novel *Luna Park*[21] play as important a role in *Blanche ou l'oubli* as do any of the characters. According to Aragon, the novel is an inexhaustible source of knowledge whose function is to teach, and the most important lesson taught by the novel is the lesson of love. While the loose, ambiguous form of *Blanche ou l'oubli*, as well as of *La Mise à mort*, represents an innovation in the form of the novel, the protagonist of both is, as in all of Aragon's novels, love. Both works bear witness to Aragon's constant belief that "man's greatest invention is love."[22]

Substituting the name of Blanche, Aragon continues in this novel his unending love song to Elsa. He writes that the day on which he met Blanche, a great distance was opened between him and many things in his past. "All the old din faded, perhaps owing to the fact that a constant music was set up in my life, a sort of accompaniment to the days and the nights. . . . Everything transpired as if I had new lips, another body, a reason for living, the perpetual notion of spring at the back of my mind. I had met that woman, my wife, that is why."[23] Gaiffier states that all that he writes in this endless series of pages is an attempt to recapture the time when they were together, when "language was an hour glass that one inverted so that the sand of words passed from one to the other, and then, from the other back again . . ."[24]

He writes that his story is perhaps the story of all men who truly love a woman and whose passion reveals to them all that will remain forever inacessible in the beloved. "One will never truly know what the person whom one loved, with whom one lived, slept, at times wept, really was . . . Never. The intoxication of a woman is to suddenly feel her absent, remote, different. He who has never felt that, tell me, dare tell me he loved."[25] The image of the mirror is again used in this work to symbolize the wall protecting the impenetrable recesses within each individual. Gaiffier realizes that even when he and Blanche were together and seemed to be but one person, there was always something that eluded him in his beloved.

Not only does Gaiffier seek clarification of his personal life, he also seeks insight into the lives of others. What he calls the hypothesis of Blanche is intended to lead the reader to see vast parts of the world in which he lives, so that he will no longer be content to limit himself to the tiny, restricted sphere of his own life. Just as Flaubert's *Education sentimentale* opens a window onto the Revolution of 1848, and Holderlin's *Hyperion* illuminates the Greek War of Independence, so does Aragon's novel reveal what he calls the "décor" of Blanche, from Guernica to Vietnam and Indonesia. It is the novel that teaches the art of living and dying. Science has as yet been unable to integrate into its classifications the human experience. At the end of all scientific analysis there remains a residue which cannot be analyzed, and that is man. What eludes science in this domain, Aragon calls the novel, and man is the matter of which the novel is constituted. The novel will retain its importance until the time comes when variations in human nature can be measured, and we know "by how many light seconds man's despair has been modified, and how to correct in him the ecliptic displacement of night and suffering."[26]

The goal of the novel is to return man to the mental framework of childhood, a period during which the child refuses to accept conclusions and always wishes to know more. Aragon wants his novel to force the reader to think beyond what he has read, to stimulate him to ask questions. In this way, the novel will serve to change those who read it. What is characteristic of great novels is their ability to make the person who has read them want to go beyond them. A good novel has the ability to open up what Aragon calls "chains of thought." These chains greatly resemble the sacrilegious chain letters of prayer in which an individual somewhere writes a prayer and sends it by mail to someone else, instructing him to copy it and send it along to others who, in turn, will do the same under threat of dire consequences to the one who interrupts the chain. The novel, too, is passed along and the one who "recopies it" or dreams about it, recognizes its power and its mission. Thus, by his novel, the author stimulates an endless series of questions, permitting the infinite to enter into what seemed only to be a limited human experience, and awakens within his readers the principle upon which all science is based—the principle of doubt.

For the novelist, writing is a form of thinking. It is also a means of struggling against forgetfulness. As Gaiffier struggles to remember his moments with Blanche, he is less moved by what he remembers than by what he has forgotten. If he tries to reconstitute a situation in the past, it is not because he has forgotten it, it merely eludes him. Should he attempt to force himself to remember it, he starts to imagine it, and imagining is the greatest form of forgetfulness. It is worse than no thought at all, since it represents thought occupied elsewhere than in reality. "Life, for the inner eye which seeks to reconstitute it, greatly resembles those dreams you think you remember, but which are then impossible to pin down exactly . . . I reread my life like a novel that I might have liked, or not liked, in short which formerly made a certain impression on me. . . . Is that forgetting? A game of hide and seek with oneself. There are entire periods of one's existence that seem lost in this way."[27]

Aragon's progressive disillusionment with Marxism again is reflected here, as he remarks that he was one of those who firmly believed that it was enough to change the economic basis of society to make theft, murder, and unhappy love disappear. This was because the idea we have of things does not necessarily take into account the complexity of life. In *Blanche ou l'oubli*, Aragon writes that he has spent his life trying to imagine the world other than it is, but to no avail. Civil strife erupts in Indonesia, and then, "just like that, indifferently, a million men are killed along the roads somewhere."[28]

In this novel, Aragon attempts to formulate a new theory of language. He states that the novel is written in a language in which words say more, less, or different things from their dictionary definitions. Life goes by, and words become emptied of their original meaning. They still maintain a vague contact with reality, but there is nothing inside them. So many words have different meanings from those they had in the author's youth. When he was a child, *voiture* (car) referred to a horse-drawn carriage. With the advent of the automobile, they said an automobile car, or even an automobile. But today, car always means an automobile; the horse has been forgotten. Life is like that—things change and the words remain. The novel represents the moment in which the word has shed its original meaning and has not yet taken on a new one, a moment of marvelous liberty and infinite linguistic possibilities. These words, continues Aragon, are my tools, "I perform by words, in words, a sort of vivisection of man."[29]

His novel, writes Aragon, is a meditation on life that is formed at the level of his awareness of the world, at the level of language. It is an enormous semantic unity that makes life possible for him and which he finds indispensable. A novel is language organized by him, an entity that permits him to live. Thus, in *Blanche ou l'oubli*, the cycle started in 1919 is completed. To palliate the despair occasioned by the horrors of war and the bankruptcy of modern civilization, the Surrealist Aragon had proposed the magic of words and love. When, almost fifty years later, he cries out—"How can we bear the world as it is?"[30]—the answer is still supplied by literary creativity and love.

CHAPTER 7

Conclusion

Aragon's evolution as a writer has been characterized by the search for the meaning of man's existence. While the answers he has proposed have varied, his quest has remained constant. He has stated that he writes to learn and to communicate what he has learned to others, not in detailed form or in the form of a scientific treatise, but through "the short cut of the image, the short cut of poetry, which offers all possibilities, all ramifications of knowledge."[1] Aragon believes that writing is the highest form of expression and that what has been written, whether novel or poetry, is, in a sense, a letter which breaks down seemingly insurmountable barriers between people or nations. It is his writing that makes the world bearable for the author, both because it serves him as a means of confession and because he creates a new way of thinking that can be followed by others.

This concept of literature as means of rendering service to mankind has been dominant throughout Aragon's work. He has sought to transform mankind through his writing, adopting Gorky's definition of the goal of literature, which is to "help man to understand himself, to exalt his faith in himself and to increase within him the desire for truth, the desire to struggle against the baseness of man and to know how to find what is good in them, to awaken in their souls shame, anger, bravery, to do everything possible to make men acquire a noble vigor and to bring down into their lives the Holy Spirit of beauty."[2]

Because of his Marxist beliefs, most of Aragon's writing has been free of the existential anguish characterizing so much twentieth-century literature. The Marxist universe is an objective world in which every action has meaning and where the belief in human progress precludes cosmic preoccupations. Recently, however, Aragon has expressed increasing doubt about the possibility of transforming the world through Socialist Realism:

> For so long did I believe I could transform into
>   gold
> All that I touched with a wing or a word
> For so long did I believe that I had the force
> That I had the alcohol that I was the flame
> And sometimes sometimes I still believe it[3]

Instead, he has returned to the eternal theme of the tragedy of human existence. Even if he is unable to transform mankind completely, Aragon believes that he can justify his existence by literary creativity: ". . . if I have only brought to light . . . the tragedy of our destiny . . . then I will perhaps have been useful for something, and one day, one day, they will breathe a sort of sympathy for me, which is all that I ask. I will have served, understand that well."[4]

To make bearable the tragedy of human existence, Aragon proposes, for himself, writing, and, for all of mankind, love. Love, which is both a gift and a choice, is the justification of man's existence. It is the explanation of his destiny and the key to his future. "If I have learned only one thing in this life," he writes, "it is to love. And I can wish you nothing more than to know how to love."[5]

Aragon has excelled in various genres during different periods of his career. In his early, Surrealist days, his prose works, such as *Le Paysan de Paris*, were vastly superior to his verses. Indeed, this work is one of the masterpieces of French twentieth-century literature. During the 1930s, Aragon's major achievements were the novels of "Le Monde réel," which painted a revealing fresco of French society at the turn of the century. His poetry of this period, published in the collections *Persécuté persécuteur*, *Hourra l'Oural*, and *La Grande Gaieté*, like his later novel *Les Communistes*, subordinated the esthetic to the political and, as a result, have suffered the fate of thesis literature. It was not until the 1940s that Aragon was to write the poems that are among the finest written in the French language. While the verses of this period and the following ten years sing of Aragon's love for his wife and country with great power and beauty, his short stories dealing with the same themes seem almost artless and naïve in comparison. *La Semaine sainte*, published in 1958, inaugurated a new series of prose works. This novel, as well as *La Mise à mort* and *Blanche ou l'oubli* which followed it, re-established Aragon's reputation as a major novelist.

Aragon's literary output, spanning a period of fifty years, has been prodigious, including every genre but theater. While much of his polemic work has already become dated, his novels and verses will endure because, as one of his critics remarked, "he has breathed music into song and ballad, poem and prose, and joined words in a farandole that passes and re-passes in the memory, and reassures the heart."[6]

Notes and References

(All translations into English, unless otherwise specified, are by Lucille Becker)

Preface

1. Gaëtan Picon, *Panorama de la nouvelle littérature française* (Paris: Gallimard, 1949), p. 55.
2. *Ibid.*, p. 145.
3. Aragon, *Le Fou d'Elsa*, p. 396.
4. Aragon, *L'Enseigne de Gersaint*, p. 11.

Chapter One

1. Aragon, *Les Voyageurs de l'impériale*, p. 683.
2. Aragon, *La Lumière de Stendhal*, p. 262.
3. See Aragon, *Le Traité du style*, p. 60: "Je suis comme pas un sensible à ces pauvres mots merveilleux laissés dans notre nuit par quelques hommes que je n'ai pas connus."
4. André Breton, *Entretiens* (Paris: Gallimard, 1952), p. 31.
5. Aragon, *Littératures soviétiques*, p. 248.
6. *Ibid.*
7. *Ibid.*
8. *Le Roman inachevé*, p. 46.
9. *Ibid.*, p. 48.
10. *La Semaine sainte*, p. 326.
11. *Le Traité du style*, p. 235.
12. "J'ai fait le mouvement Dada/Disait le dadaiste/J'ai fait le mouvement Dada/Et en effet/Il l'avait fait."
13. Maurice Nadeau, *The History of Surrealism* (Translated from the French by Richard Howard, New York: The Macmillan Company, 1965), p. 62.
14. *Pour un réalisme socialiste*, p. 79.
15. Maurice Nadeau, *op. cit.*, p. 89.
16. *Le Roman inachevé*, p. 79.
17. *L'Homme Communiste*, Volume II, p. 188.
18. P. 245.

19. *Ibid.*, p. 218.

20. *Les Beaux Quartiers*, postface.

21. "Le Cahier noir," *La Revue Européenne*, February 1, 1926, pp. 8, 11.

22. Pp. 19–20.

23. Quoted by Jean Sur in *Aragon le réalisme de l'amour* (Paris: Centurion, 1966), p. 69.

24. P. 52.

25. Maurice Nadeau, *op. cit.*, p. 101.

26. *Le Paysan de Paris*, p. 79.

27. See Maurice Nadeau, *op. cit.*, p. 289.

28. *Pour un réalisme socialiste*, p. 16.

29. See Maurice Nadeau, *op. cit.*, p. 290.

30. *Ibid.*, p. 288.

31. *Ibid.*, p. 180.

32. P. 85.

33. *J'Abats mon jeu*, p. 28.

34. Quoted by Aragon in *Journal d'une poésie nationale*, p. 15.

35. *Pour un réalisme socialiste*, p. 55.

36. *Les Beaux Quartiers*, postface.

37. Gaëtan Picon, *op. cit.*, p. 57.

38. *Littératures soviétiques*, p. 24.

39. *Les Yeux et la mémoire*, p. 36.

40. *Ibid.*, p. 19.

41. *J'Abats mon jeu*, p. 134.

Chapter Two

1. "Secousse," "Le monde à bas je le bâtis plus beau."

2. "Novembre."

3. "Lever."

4. *Ibid.*

5. *Ibid.*

6. "Pour demain."

7. "Fugue."

8. *Le Libertinage*, p. 8.

9. "Air du Temps," *Le Mouvement perpétuel*, p. 26.

10. "Une Vague de rêves," *Commerce*, Autumn 1924, p. 105.

11. Quoted by Maurice Nadeau, *op. cit.*, pp. 83–84.

12. "Une Vague de rêves," p. 100.

13. André Breton, *Manifeste du surréalisme* (Paris: Editions Kra, 1924), p. 63.

14. "Serrure de Sûreté," *Le Mouvement perpétuel*, p. 23.

15. "Une Vague de rêves," p. 93.

16. "De l'exactitude historique en poésie," *En étrange pays dans mon pays lui-même*, p. 32.

17. *Traité du style*, p. 187.
18. *Ibid.*, p. 189.
19. *Anicet ou le Panorama roman*, p. 36.
20. *Ibid.*, p. 15.
21. *Ibid.*, p. 21.
22. *Ibid.*, p. 26.
23. *Ibid.*, p. 27.
24. *Ibid.*, p. 55.
25. *Ibid.*, p. 69.
26. *Ibid.*, p. 8.
27. *Ibid.*, p. 75.
28. *Ibid.*, p. 139.
29. *Ibid.*, pp. 125−26.
30. *Les Aventures de Télémaque*, pp. 28−29.
31. *Ibid.*, pp. 36−37.
32. *Ibid.*, p. 98.
33. *Ibid.*, p. 100.
34. *Ibid.*, p. 101.
35. *Le Libertinage*, p. 8.
36. *Ibid.*, p. 9.
37. *Ibid.*, p. 56.
38. *Ibid.*, p. 61.
39. *En étrange pays dans mon pays lui-même*, "Le Paysan de Paris chante," p.44.
40. *Le Paysan de Paris*, p. 10.
41. *Ibid.*, pp. 13−14.
42. *Ibid.*, p. 19.
43. *Ibid.*, p. 59.
44. *Ibid.*, p. 80.
45. *Ibid.*, p. 245.
46. *Ibid.*, p. 79.
47. *Ibid.*, p. 209.
48. *Ibid.*, p. 249.
49. Maurice Nadeau, *op. cit.*, Preface by Roger Shattuck, p. 22.
50. Text from a catalogue for an exhibition of collages, 1930.
51. *Pour un réalisme socialiste*, a collection of lectures given by Aragon from April to June 1935, p. 52.
52. Quoted in Maurice Nadeau, *op.cit.*, p. 25.
53. "Chronique de la pluie et du beau temps," *Europe*, April, 1947, p. 104.
54. Quoted in Maurice Nadeau, *op. cit.*, p. 285.
55. *Ibid.*, p. 288.
56. *Persécuté persécuteur*, p. 24.
57. *Ibid.*, p. 64.
58. *Hourra l'Oural*, p. 28.

59. *Ibid.*, p. 51.
60. *Ibid.*, p. 137.

Chapter Three

1. Quoted in *Aragon Poet of the French Resistance*, edited by Hannah Josephson and Malcolm Cowley (New York: Duell, Sloan and Pearce, 1945), p. xi.
2. Ewart Milne in *Poems for France* as quoted by Claude Roy, *Aragon* (Paris: Seghers, 1962), p. 7.
3. *L'Homme Communiste*, I, p. 84.
4. *Le Crève-coeur*, "Vingt ans après," p. 10.
5. *Ibid.*, "La Valse des vingt ans," p. 27.
6. *Ibid.*, "Les Lilas et les roses," pp. 45–46.
"O mois des floraisons mois des métamorphoses/Mai qui fut sans nuage et Juin poignardé/Je n'oublierai jamais les lilas ni les roses/Ni ceux que le printemps dans ses plis a gardés . . . Je n'oublierai jamais les jardins de la France/Semblables aux missels des siècles disparus/Ni le trouble des soirs l'énigme du silence/Les roses tout le long du chemin parcouru/Le démenti des fleurs au vent de la panique/Aux soldats qui passaient sur l'aile de la peur . . . On nous a dit ce soir que Paris s'est rendu/Je n'oublierai jamais les lilas ni les roses/Et ni les deux amours que nous avons perdus."
7. Act IV, Scene 1: "You may my glories and my state depose/But not my griefs; still am I king of those."
8. *Le Crève-coeur*, "Richard II Quarante," p. 56.
9. *Ibid.*, "Zone Libre," p. 59.
10. *Littératures soviétiques*, p. 324.
11. Pp. 75–76.
12. These poems were inspired by *Les Nuits* of Alfred de Musset.
13. *Les Yeux d'Elsa*, "La Nuit d'Exil," p. 29.
"Ces nuits t'en souvient-il Me souvenir me nuit/Avaient autant d'éclairs que l'oeil noir des colombes/Rien ne nous reste plus de ces bijoux de l'ombre/Nous savons maintenant ce que c'est que la nuit . . . Reverrons-nous jamais le paradis lointain/Les Halles l'Opéra la Concorde et le Louvre/Ces nuits t'en souvient-il quand la nuit nous recouvre/La nuit qui vient du coeur et n'a pas de matin."
14. *Ibid.*, "Plus belle que les larmes," p. 58.
15. *Ibid.*, p. 62.
16. *Ibid.*, "Elsa-Valse," p. 88.
17. "Arma virumque cano," Preface to *Les Yeux d'Elsa*, p. 22.
18. *Le Musée Grévin*, p. 7.
19. *Ibid.*, p. 23.
20. *Ibid.*, p. 10.
21. *Ibid.*, p. 28.
22. *Ibid.*

23. Vast forest in Bretagne in which the novels of the Round Table placed the dwelling of the magician Merlin.
24. "De l'exactitude historique en poésie," p. 28.
25. *Ibid.*, p. 36.
26. *La Diane française*, pp. 24–26.
27. *En Français dans le texte*, p. 43.
28. "O mares sur la terre au soir de mon pays," *La Diane française*, pp. 16–17.
29. *La Diane française*, pp. 72, 74.
30. *Ibid.*, "Ballade de celui qui chanta dans les supplices," p. 43.
31. *Ibid.*, pp. 43–45.
32. *Ibid.*, p. 27.
33. *Ibid.*, p. 83.
34. *Chroniques du bel canto*, pp. 79–80.
35. *Ibid.*, p. 246.

Chapter Four

1. *J'Abats mon jeu*, pp. 75–76.
2. *Les Cloches de Bâle*, p. 247.
3. *Ibid.*, pp. 87–88.
4. *Ibid.*, p. 103.
5. *Ibid.*, pp. 168–69.
6. *J'Abats mon jeu*, p. 92.
7. *Les Cloches de Bâle*, p. 424.
8. *Ibid.*, pp. 421–22.
9. *Ibid.*, p. 438.
10. David Caute, *Communism and the French Intellectuals* (New York: Macmillan Company, 1964), p. 322.
11. *L'Exemple de Courbet*, pp. 15, 39.
12. This is a critical work containing various prefaces devoted to Prosper Mérimée, Heinrich von Kleist, Marceline Desbordes-Valmore, Jules de la Madelène, etc., and scientific criticism of the works of Webster, Merle, Zola, Barrès, Stendhal, based on the methods of socialist realism.
13. *La Lumière de Stendhal*, p. 56.
14. *J'Abats mon jeu*, p. 268.
15. P. 465.
16. P. 11.
17. *Les Cloches de Bâle*, p. 287.
18. *Les Beaux Quartiers*, p. 69.
19. *Ibid.*, p. 164.
20. *Ibid.*, pp. 172–73.
21. *Ibid.*, p. 242.
22. *Littératures soviétiques*, p. 358.
23. *L'Homme Communiste*, I, pp. 42–43.

24. *Anicet*, p. 110.

25. *Le Paysan de Paris*, p. 234.

26. *Les Beaux Quartiers*, p. 462.

27. This novel was translated into English as *The Century was Young*. Translated literally, it means "Those who Travel on the Outside Platform of the Bus."

28. *Les Voyageurs de l'impériale*, p. 626.

29. "Aragon répond à ses critiques," *La Nouvelle Critique*, No. 8, June 17, 1949, p. 83.

30. *Les Voyageurs de l'impériale*, p. 275.

31. *Ibid.*, p. 393.

32. *Ibid.*, p. 693.

33. *Ibid.*, p. 694.

34. *Le Nouveau Crève-coeur*, p. 85.

35. *Les Voyageurs de l'impériale*, p. 240.

36. *Ibid.*, pp. 519−20.

37. *Aurélien*, p. 9.

38. *Ibid.*, pp. 295−96.

39. *Ibid.*, p. 465.

40. *Ibid.*, p. 697.

41. *Les Communistes*, IV, p. 187.

42. *Ibid.*, VI, p. 322.

43. *Ibid.*, p. 340.

44. *La Semaine sainte*, p. 461.

45. *J'Abats mon jeu*, p. 73.

46. *La Semaine sainte*, p. 323.

47. *Ibid.*, p. 330.

48. From *Holy Week*, translated by Haakon Chevalier (New York: Popular Library, 1962), p. 420. In *La Semaine sainte*, pp. 466−67.

49. *Holy Week*, p. 314. *La Semaine sainte*, pp. 341−42.

50. *J'Abats mon jeu*, p. 69.

51. *L'Homme Communiste*, I, p. 67.

52. *La Semaine sainte*, p. 100.

53. *Holy Week*, pp. 529−30. *La Semaine sainte*, pp. 583−84.

54. *Holy Week*, p. 529. *La Semaine sainte*, p. 583.

55. "La peinture au défi," in *Les Collages*, pp. 39−40.

56. *Holy Week*, p. 543. *La Semaine sainte*, p. 597.

Chapter Five

1. *J'Abats mon jeu*, p. 132.

2. *Les Yeux et la mémoire*, p. 27. "Et tu vins en novembre et sur quelques paroles/Ma vie a tout d'un coup tout autrement tourné/Un soir

au bar de la Coupole//Avant toi je n'étais qu'une ombre inassouvie/L'errement de moi-même aveugle et sourd/Tu m'aurais tout appris lumière de ma vie/Jusqu'à voir la couleur du jour//Toi qui rouvris pour moi le ciel de la bonté/En moi qui réveillas les musiques profondes/Toi qui m'as fait moi-même et m'as dit de chanter/Comme un enfant devant le monde."

3. Introduction to *Poésies Anthologie 1917–1960* (Paris: Club du meilleur livre, 1960).

4. *Le Crève-coeur*, p. 20.

5. *Ibid.*, "Vingt ans après," p. 11. "O mon amour o mon amour toi seule existe/A cette heure pour moi du crépuscule triste/Où je perds à la fois le fil de mon poème/Et celui de ma vie et la joie et la voix/Parce que j'ai voulu te redire Je t'aime/Et que ce mot fait mal quand il est dit sans toi."

6. *Ibid.*, "Le Printemps," p. 37. "Rendez-moi rendez-moi mon ciel et ma musique/Ma femme sans qui rien n'a chanson ni couleur/Sans qui Mai n'est pour moi que le désert physique/Le soleil qu'une insulte et l'ombre une douleur."

7. *La Diane française*, "Il n'y a pas d'amour heureux," p. 35. "Mon bel amour mon cher amour ma déchirure/Je te porte dans moi comme un oiseau blessé/. . . . Le temps d'apprendre à vivre il est déjà trop tard/Que pleurent dans la nuit nos coeurs à l'unisson/Ce qu'il faut de malheur pour la moindre chanson/Ce qu'il faut de regrets pour payer un frisson/Ce qu'il faut de sanglots pour un air de guitare//Il n'y a pas d'amour qui ne soit à douleur/Il n'y a pas d'amour dont on ne soit meurtri/Il n'y a pas d'amour dont on ne soit flétri/Et pas plus que de toi l'amour de la patrie/Il n'y a pas d'amour qui ne vive de pleurs/Il n'y a pas d'amour heureux/Mais c'est notre amour à tous deux."

8. *Entretiens avec Francis Crémieux*, p. 100.

9. *Aurélien*, p. 233.

10. *Le Crève-coeur*, p. 66. "Au biseau des baisers/Les ans passent trop vite/Evite évite évite/Les souvenirs brisés."

11. *Ibid.*, p. 67. "La vie aura coulé sans qu'on y prenne garde."

12. "Cantique à Elsa," *Les Yeux d'Elsa*, pp. 68–69. "Jamais rassasié de ces yeux qui m'affament/Mon ciel mon désespoir ma femme/. . . . J'aurais tremblé treize ans sur le seuil des chimères/Treize ans d'une peur douce-amère/Et treize ans conjuré des périls inventés//O mon enfant le temps n'est pas à notre taille/Que mille et une nuits sont peu pour des amants/Treize ans c'est comme un jour et c'est un feu de paille/Qui brûle à nos pieds maille à maille/Le magique tapis de notre isolement."

13. "Les Yeux d'Elsa," *Les Yeux d'Elsa*, p. 24. "Il advint qu'un beau soir l'univers se brisa/Sur des récifs que les naufrageurs enflammèrent/Moi je voyais briller au-dessus de la mer/Les yeux d'Elsa les yeux d'Elsa les yeux d'Elsa."

14. "Cantique à Elsa," *Les Yeux d'Elsa*, p. 70. "Tant pis si le bateau des étoiles chavire/Puisqu'il porte ton nom larguez larguez les ris/On le verra briller au grand mât du navire/Alors Hélène Laure Elvire/Sortiront t'accueillir comme un mois de Marie."

15. "Lancelot," *Les Yeux d'Elsa*, p. 65. "Je suis ce chevalier qu'on dit de la charrette/Qui si l'amour le mène ignore ce qu'il craint."

16. "Arma virumque cano," *Les Yeux d'Elsa*, pp. 21–22. "Mon Amour: On dira qu'un homme se doit de ne pas exposer son amour sur la place publique. Je répondrai qu'un homme n'a rien de meilleur, de plus pur, et de plus digne d'être perpétué que son amour qui est cette musique même dont parle Portia, et que c'est lâcheté et faiblesse de craindre porter son amour au pavois. Je veux qu'un jour vienne où, regardant notre nuit, les gens y voient pourtant briller une flamme, et quelle flamme puis-je aviver sinon celle qui est en moi? Mon amour, tu est ma seule famille avouée, et je vois par tes yeux le monde, c'est toi qui me rends cet univers sensible et qui donnes sens en moi aux sentiments humains."

17. *Les Yeux d'Elsa*, p. 44.

18. "Cantique à Elsa," *Les Yeux d'Elsa*, p. 75. "Si tu veux que je t'aime apporte-moi l'eau pure/A laquelle s'en vont leurs désirs s'étancher. . . . //Que ton poème soit l'espoir qui dit A suivre/Au bas du feuilleton sinistre de nos pas/Que triomphe la voix humaine sur les cuivres/Et donne une raison de vivre/A ceux que tout semblait inviter au trépas."

19. *Chroniques du bel canto*, pp. 52, 54, 55. ". . . il y a dans la poésie moderne cette nouveauté sur quoi, au nom du platonisme éternel, on ne saurait nous faire revenir, c'est que l'homme n'est plus pensé sans la femme, ni la femme sans l'homme, et que la haute expression de l'amour de ce temps, ce n'est plus une *idée* de l'amour . . . mais le couple . . . lorsque l'homme et la femme s'élèvent simultanément à une même conception du monde, où leur aventure s'élargit, et l'amour au devenir humain s'identifie."

20. *Les Communistes*, II, p. 93.

21. *Ibid.*, IV, p. 119.

22. *Ibid.*

23. *Ibid.*, pp. 341–42. ". . . cette douceur de l'homme et de la femme à qui le monde n'est point limité tant qu'ils sont mêlés, leurs haleines et leurs corps, leur exaltation et leur repos. Ils parlent doucement dans la nuit très tard, et leurs pensées sont entrelacées comme une tresse de bonheur; de tous côtés, ils se prolongent vers cet avenir qui est en eux, et qui ne peut être que de leur rapprochement. . . . Cette expérience n'est point transmissible. Ceux-là qui la font, seuls et dans ce seul moment qu'ils la font, en éprouvent à la fois le vertige et la profondeur merveilleuse."

24. Quoted in Jean Sur, *Aragon le réalisme de l'amour*, p. 80.

25. *Ibid.*, p. 161.

26. *Les Yeux et la mémoire*, p. 11. "Mon amour à la fin du monde/Ah qu'au moins ma voix te réponde."

27. *Ibid.*, p. 15. "Si les chants s'en vont en fumée/Que me fait que nul ne m'écoute/Les pas sont éteints sur les routes/Je continue à les rimer/Par une sorte de démence/Te répondant d'une romance/Mon seul écho ma bien-aimée."

28. *Ibid.*, p. 28. "Demeure mon amour heureux et malheureux/Demeure mon amour dans mes bras prisonnière/Soleil secret du coeur qui n'est que pour nous deux/Ma chère amour seule et dernière//Si de ce que j'écris ne restait que ton nom/Je saluerais la gloire éternelle des choses."

29. *Ibid.*, p. 147. "Homme et femme à la fin si les coeurs font la paire/L'histoire et leur amour étroitement les nouent/Ils espèrent ensemble ensemble désespèrent/Ils se dressent ensemble ou tombent à genoux//Le couple est comme un peuple uni."

30. *Ibid.*, p. 139.

31. *Ibid.*, p. 141. "Rien ne fait l'homme et la femme si grands/Que cet amour l'un l'autre qui les prend/Heureux les gens un jour pareils à ceux qui s'aiment/Dans un univers différent."

32. *Ibid.*, p. 30. "Est-ce un crime vraiment de dire ce qu'on voit/Partager son amour chanter chercher des rimes/Je ne sais pas vraiment ce que l'on veut de moi/Est-ce vraiment vraiment un crime//De rêver au bonheur dans la gueule du loup/Et de dire à minuit que l'alouette est proche/Mes amis mes amis que cela soit de vous/Pourtant qu'en vienne le reproche//Le paysage Allez je sais ce que l'on dit/*Il faut peindre l'histoire il faut peindre la lutte*/Et que nous venez-vous en pleine tragédie/Jouer un petit air de flûte."

33. *Ibid.*, pp. 36–37. "Je réclame le droit de rêver au tournant/De la route Aux grands charmes de la promenade/Le droit de m'émouvoir du monde maintenant/Que s'approche la cannonade/ . . . Je réclame le droit de croire au lendemain/De croire à la musique au bonheur au décor/Au grand soleil qui fait aux arbres du chemin/Danser pour nous des feuilles d'or."

34. *Ibid.*, pp. 97–98. "Et je songeais qu'un jour pareil dans pas long-temps/Je ne reviendrai plus vers toi le coeur battant/ . . . Je ne toucherai plus ta chevelure au soir/Je ne souffrirai pas de ne jamais te voir//Je ne sentirai plus le coeur me palpiter/Pour un mot de ta voix dans la chambre à côté."

35. *Ibid.*, pp. 20–21. "C'est une chose au fond que je ne puis comprendre/Cette peur de mourir que les gens ont en eux/Comme si ce n'était

pas assez merveilleux/Que le ciel un moment nous ait paru si tendre/. . . . Malgré la guerre et l'injustice et l'insomnie/Où l'on porte rongeant votre coeur ce renard/L'amertume et Dieu sait si je l'ai pour ma part/Porté comme un enfant volé toute ma vie/. . . . Malgré tout je vous dis que cette vie fut telle/Qu'à qui voudra m'entendre à qui je parle ici/N'ayant plus sur la lèvre un seul mot que merci/Je dirai malgré tout que cette vie fut belle."

36. *Le Roman inachevé*, p. 13. "Vous sentez dans vos bras tout à coup la dimension du monde/Et votre propre force et que tout est possible soudain."

37. *Ibid.*, pp. 81, 83. "Ici commence la grande nuit des mots/Ici le nom se détache de ce qu'il nomme/. . . . Voilà cela commence comme cela les mots vous mènent/On perd de vue les toits on perd de vue la terre On suit/Inexplicablement le chemin des oiseaux."

38. *Ibid.*, pp. 100, 103–4. "Un amour qui commence est le pays d'au-delà le miroir/. . . . Une femme c'est une porte qui s'ouvre sur l'inconnu/Une femme cela vous envahit comme chante une source/On quitte tout pour une femme et tout prend une autre envergure/Tout s'harmonise avec sa voix La femme c'est le Merveilleux/Tout à ses pas se transfigure."

39. *Ibid.*, pp. 173, 182. "Ma vie en vérité commence/Le jour où je t'ai rencontré/. . . . Et la vie a passé le temps d'un éclair au ciel sillonné/ J'écoute au fin fond de moi le bruit de mes propres pas s'éteindre/. . . . Il me semble qu'il n'y a eu que mon amour dans l'existence//Je n'ai rien fait que par toi que pour toi pour l'amour de toi."

40. *Ibid.*, p. 34.

41. *Ibid.*, "Le Vieil Homme," p. 168. "Je ne tiens plus jamais jamais entre mes bras/La mer qui se ruait et me roulait d'écume/Jusqu'à ce qu'à la fin tous les deux fussions las//Voilà déjà beau temps que je n'ai plus coutume/De défier la neige et gravir les sommets/Dans l'éblouissement du soleil et des brumes."

42. *Ibid.*, p. 236. "Où tu vas je te suis La vie est ton sillage/Je te tiens contre moi Tout le reste est mirage/. . . . Non je n'ai jamais mal quand je t'ai dans mes bras//C'est par toi que je vis Elsa de ma jeunesse//Que serais-je sans toi qu'un homme à la dérive."

43. *Elsa*, pp. 90, 93. "Toi qui es la rose ô mystérieuse rose en ce temps de l'année/. . . . Où tout n'est qu'oraison de ta gloire et de ta semblance/O rose qui est ton être et ton nom//*J'inventerai pour toi la rose.*"

44. *Ibid.*, p. 79. "O beauté finissant ô beauté plus belle de finir/O mon amour beau comme le bout de l'année/O rose du bout de l'année."

45. *Ibid.*, p. 13. "Voilà devant moi la grande vérité de l'hiver/Tout homme a le destin de l'étincelle Tout homme n'est/Qu'une éphémère et que suis-je de plus que tout homme/Mon orgueil est d'avoir aimé//Rien

d'autre//Et la pierre s'enfonce sans fin dans la poussière des planètes/Je ne suis qu'un peu de vin renversé mais le vin/Témoigne de l'ivresse au petit matin blême//Rien d'autre//J'étais né pour ces mots que j'ai dits//Mon amour."

46. *Ibid.*, p. 113. "Quand tu dors dans mes bras je peux longuement caresser ton âme."

47. *Ibid.*, p. 19. "L'Ave sans fin des litanies/Ma perpétuelle insomnie/Ma floraison mon embellie/O ma raison ô ma folie/Mon mois de mai ma mélodie/Mon paradis mon incendie//Mon univers Elsa ma vie."

48. *Ibid.*, p. 20.

49. *Ibid.*, pp. 36–39.

50. *Ibid.*, p. 61.

51. *Ibid.*, p. 124. "Un jour Elsa mes vers qui seront ta couronne/Et qui me survivront d'être par toi portés/On les comprendra mieux dans leur diversité/Par ce reflet de toi que tes cheveux leur donnent/Un jour Elsa mes vers en raison de tes yeux/De tes yeux pénétrants et doux qui surent voir/Demain comme personne aux derniers feux du soir/Un jour Elsa mes vers on les comprendra mieux/. . . ."

52. *Les Poètes*, p. 133. "Un poète est celui qui fait des poèmes/Un poème est la forme que prend la poésie/Mais qu'est-ce que c'est qu'est-ce que c'est la poésie//Cette chose en moi cette chose en dehors de moi."

53. *Ibid.*, p. 46. "Je paye moins pour le feu donné aux hommes/Que pour cette espérance dans leur oeil et dans leurs bras la vie/Comme une femme/Demain comme un enfant/Je paye pour avoir donné la certitude à l'homme/Qu'il fait le monde à son image//. . . . Je paye pour ce que fait l'homme sans limite."

54. *Ibid.*, p. 152.

55. *Ibid.*, p. 22. "Je suis arrivé sans même le remarquer à cette extrémité de moi-même/A ce point d'où tu ne peux que regarder en arrière parce qu'il n'y a plus rien devant toi."

56. *Ibid.*, p. 161. "Le monde est mal fait mon coeur las/ . . . Faute de vaillance ou d'audace/Tout va son train rien n'a changé/On s'arrange avec le danger/L'âge vient sans que rien se passe."

57. *Ibid.*, p. 173. "Le ciel en moi des mots son scintillement vague/Cette multitude étoilée en moi/Je n'en ai pas fini de m'émerveiller des mots De cette nuit/Des mots en moi De cette poussière en moi d'un long dimanche /Cette lumière à l'infini divisée et qui m'expliquera/Les étranges accouplements de leurs kaléidoscopies/La collision des couleurs les architectures du chant//Cosmos intérieur beau comme les mains jointes/Je n'en ai pas je n'en aurais jamais fini de m'émerveiller/De ces formations de cristaux de ces précipitations de la parole."

58. *Ibid.*, p. 182. "Musique de ma vie ô mon parfum ma femme/ Empare-toi de moi jusqu'au profond de l'âme//Entre dans mon poème unique passion/Qu'il soit uniquement ta respiration//Immobile sans toi désert de ton absence/Qu'il prenne enfin de toi son sens et sa puissance."

59. *Ibid.*, p. 193.

60. *Il ne m'est Paris que d'Elsa*, p. 10.

61. *Ibid.*, p. 18.

62. *Ibid.*, p. 28.

63. *Ibid.*, p. 83.

64. *Ibid.*, p. 167.

65. *Le Voyage de Hollande*, p. 34. "Il n'est à voir que ton visage/ Entendre que ta voix aimée/Car soient mes yeux ou non fermés/Je n'ai que toi de paysage/. . . . Breughel d'Enfer ou de Velours/Moulins tulipes diableries/N'est Hollande à ma songerie/Que mon amour que mon amour."

66. *Le Fou d'Elsa*, pp. 14–15.

67. *Ibid.*, p. 15.

68. *Ibid.*, pp. 13–14.

69. *Ibid.*, p. 58.

70. *Ibid.*, p. 62.

71. *Ibid.*, p. 98.

72. *Ibid.*, p. 78. "Que ce soit dimanche ou lundi/Soir ou matin minuit midi/Dans l'enfer ou le paradis/Les amours aux amours se ressemblent/ C'était hier que je t'ai dit/*Nous dormirons ensemble*// C'était hier et c'est demain/Je n'ai plus que toi de chemin/J'ai mis mon coeur entre tes mains/Avec le tien comme il va l'amble/Tout ce qu'il y a de temps humain/*Nous dormirons ensemble*//Mon amour ce qui fut sera/Le ciel est sur nous comme un drap/J'ai refermé sur toi mes bras/Et tant je t'aime que j'en tremble/Aussi longtemps que tu voudras/*Nous dormirons ensemble*."

73. *Ibid.*, p. 145.

74. *Ibid.*, p. 166. "L'avenir de l'homme est la femme/Elle est la couleur de son âme/Elle est sa rumeur et son bruit/Et sans elle il n'est qu'un blasphème/Il n'est qu'un noyau sans le fruit/. . . . Je vous dis que l'homme est né pour/La femme et né pour l'amour/Tout du monde ancien va changer/D'abord la vie et puis la mort/Et toutes choses partagées/Le pain blanc les baisers qui saignent/On verra le couple et son règne/Neiger comme les orangers."

75. *Ibid.*, p. 355.

76. *Ibid.*, p. 361.

77. *Ibid.*, p. 385.

78. *Ibid.*, p. 92. "Cette vie elle s'achève/Amour mon seul absolu/Pour

toi des soleils se lèvent/Qui crépuscules n'ont plus/Cette vie est longue et brève/Amour d'au-delà des rêves."

Chapter Six

1. *J'Abats mon jeu*, p. 20.
2. Frontispiece, *La Mise à mort*.
3. *Ibid.*, p. 232.
4. *Ibid.*, p. 195.
5. Lewis Carroll, *Through the Looking Glass*, p. 149.
6. *La Mise à mort*, p. 156.
7. *Elsa*, p. 64.
8. *La Mise à mort*, p. 130.
9. *La Diane française*, pp. 37–38.
10. *Le Fou d'Elsa*, p. 185.
11. *Ibid.*, p. 201.
12. *La Mise à mort*, pp. 33–34.
13. *Ibid.*, p. 67.
14. *Ibid.*, p. 68.
15. *Ibid.*, p. 398.
16. *Ibid.*, p. 421.
17. *Ibid.*, p. 57.
18. *Ibid.*, p. 58.
19. *Ibid.*, pp. 405–6.
20. *Blanche ou l'oubli*, p. 482.
21. The heroine of Elsa's novel *Luna Park*, Blanche Hauteville, who lends her name to the heroine of Aragon's novel, is an aviatrix who has disappeared over the Sahara. A young director, resting between films, has rented the house of this woman he has never met. One day, he finds packages of letters in a desk drawer which he is irresistibly drawn to read. All are love letters, and from different men, each of whom describes her differently, as he saw her, so that the young director is unable to form a comprehensive image of her.
22. *Blanche ou l'oubli*, p. 300.
23. *Ibid.*, p. 60.
24. *Ibid.*, p. 395.
25. *Ibid.*, p. 473.
26. *Ibid.*, p. 213.
27. *Ibid.*, p. 41.
28. *Ibid.*, p. 512.

29. *Ibid.*, p. 360.
30. *Ibid.*, p. 512.

Chapter Seven

1. *Entretiens avec Francis Crémieux*, p. 15.
2. *Littératures soviétiques*, p. 266.
3. *Le Fou d'Elsa*, p. 411.
4. *Les Collages*, p. 23.
5. *J'Abats mon jeu*, p. 132.
6. Dominique Arban, "Aragon at the Crossroads," *International Literary Annual*, No. 2 (1960), p. 158.

Selected Bibliography

Primary Sources

(Note: Only those works of Aragon that appeared in bound volumes are included in this bibliography. Texts in magazines and newspapers far outnumber the bound volumes. Those bound works that subsequently were incorporated into larger works are not listed. When two editions are listed, the first indicates the initial publication of the work, the second the edition mentioned in this work.)

Feu de joie. Paris: Au Sans pareil, 1920.

Anicet ou le Panorama roman. Paris: Gallimard, 1921.

Les Aventures de Télémaque. Paris: Gallimard, 1922; 1966.

Les Plaisirs de la Capitale. Berlin, 1923.

Le Libertinage. Paris: Gallimard, 1924. A short play included in this volume was translated into English by Michael Benedict as *The Mirror-Wardrobe one Fine Evening*. New York: Modern French Theater, 1964.

Une Vague de rêves. In special issue of *Commerce*, II, Autumn 1924.

Le Mouvement perpétuel. Paris: Gallimard, 1926.

Le Paysan de Paris. Paris: Gallimard, 1926; 1948.

Le Traité du style. Paris: Gallimard, 1928.

La Grande Gaieté. Paris: Gallimard, 1929.

La Peinture au défi. Paris: Editions Surréalistes, 1930.

Persécuté persécuteur. Paris: Editions Surréalistes, 1931.

Les Cloches de Bâle. Paris: Denoel et Steele, 1934. Le Livre de Poche, 1964. Trans. as *Bells of Basel* by Haakon M. Chevalier. New York: Harcourt, Brace, 1936.

Hourra l'Oural. Paris: Denoel et Steele, 1934.

Pour un réalisme socialiste. Paris: Denoel, 1935.

Les Beaux Quartiers. Paris: Denoel, 1936. Trans. as *Residential Quarter* by Haakon M. Chevalier. New York: Harcourt, Brace, 1938.

Le Crève-coeur. Paris: Gallimard, 1941.

Cantique à Elsa. Alger: Fontaine, 1941.

Les Voyageurs de l'impériale. Paris: Gallimard, 1942. Definitive edition, 1947. Le Livre de Poche, 1964. Trans. as *The Century was Young* by Hannah Josephson. New York: Duell, Sloan and Pearce, 1941.

Les Yeux d'Elsa. Neuchâtel: Les Cahiers du Rhône, 1942.

Brocéliande. Neuchâtel: Les Cahiers du Rhône, 1942.

En Français dans le texte. Paris: Ides et Calendes, 1943.

Le Musée Grévin. Paris: Editeurs Français Réunis, 1943.

Aurélien. Paris: Gallimard, 1944. Le Livre de Poche, 1964. Trans. as *Aurélien* by Eithne Wilkins. New York: Duell, Sloan and Pearce, 1947.

La Diane française. Paris: Seghers, 1945.

En Etrange pays dans mon pays lui-même (Incorporating *Brocéliande* and *En Français dans le texte*). Paris: Seghers, 1945.

Servitude et Grandeur des Français. Paris: Bibliothèque Française, 1945.

L'Enseigne de Gersaint. Paris: Ides et Calendes, 1946.

L'Homme Communiste (I). Paris: Gallimard, 1946.

Apologie du luxe. Geneva: Skira, 1946.

La Culture et les hommes. Paris: Editions Sociales, 1947.

Chroniques du bel canto. Geneva: Skira, 1947.

Le Nouveau Crève-coeur. Paris: Gallimard, 1948.

Les Communistes. Paris: Bibliothèque Française. Vol. I (Feb.–Sept., 1939), 1949; Vol. II (Sept.–Oct., 1939), 1949; Vol. III (Nov., 1939–March, 1940), 1950; Vol. IV (May, 1940), 1950; Vol. V in two volumes (May–June, 1940), 1951.

L'Exemple de Courbet. Paris: Eds. Cercle d'Art, 1952.

Hugo, poète réaliste. Paris: Editions Sociales, 1952.

Avez-vous lu Victor Hugo? Paris: Editeurs Français Réunis, 1952.

L'Homme Communiste, II. Paris: Gallimard, 1953.

Le Neveu de M. Duval. Paris: Editeurs Français Réunis, 1953.

Journal d'une poésie nationale. Lyons: Les Ecrivains Réunis, 1954.

Mes Caravanes et autres poèmes. Paris: Seghers, 1954.

La Lumière de Stendhal. Paris: Denoel, 1954.

Les Yeux et la mémoire. Paris: Gallimard, 1954.

Littératures soviétiques. Paris: Gallimard, 1955.

Introduction aux littératures soviétiques. Paris: Gallimard, 1956.

Le Roman inachevé. Paris: Gallimard, 1956.

La Semaine sainte. Paris: Gallimard, 1958. Trans. as *Holy Week* by Haakon Chevalier. New York: Popular Library, 1962.

Elsa. Paris: Gallimard, 1959.

J'Abats mon jeu. Paris: Editeurs Français Réunis, 1959.

Entretiens sur le musée de Dresde (with Jean Cocteau). Paris: Le Cercle d'Art, 1959.

Les Poètes. Paris: Gallimard, 1960.

Poésies (Anthologie 1917–60). Paris: Le Club du Meilleur Livre. 1960.

Histoire parallèle (U.R.S.S.–U.S.A.), in collaboration with André Maurois. Four volumes. Paris: Presses de la Cité, 1962. Translation of Aragon's two volumes as *A History of the U.S.S.R. from Lenin to Khrushchev* by Patrick O'Brien. London: Weidenfeld & Nicolson, 1964.

Le Fou d'Elsa. Paris: Gallimard, 1963.

Il ne m'est Paris que d'Elsa. Paris: Laffont, 1964.

Le Voyage de Hollande. Paris: Seghers, 1964.

Entretiens avec Francis Crémieux. Paris: Gallimard, 1964.

La Mise à mort. Paris: Gallimard, 1965.

Les Collages. Paris: Hermann, 1965.

Elégie à Pablo Neruda. Paris: Gallimard, 1966.

Blanche ou l'oubli. Paris: Gallimard, 1967.

Translations:

La Chasse au snark by Lewis Carroll. The Hours Press, 1928.

Cinq Sonnets de Pétrarque. A la Fontaine de Vaucluse, 1947.

Djamilia by Tchinghiz Aitmatov. Eds. Français Réunis, 1959.

Secondary Sources

(The following is a partial list of selected secondary sources.)

Albérès, René-Marrill. *La Révolte des écrivains d'aujourd'hui.* Paris: Correa, 1949. Contains a chapter on "Le Héros contre le Bovarysme— Louis Aragon," pp. 468–81. Discussion of the refusal of Aragon's heroes to compromise their ideals.

Anglès, Auguste. "Aragon est aussi un romancier," *Problèmes du roman* under the direction of Jean Prévost. Lyons, *Confluences*, 1943. Discussion of *Les Cloches de Bâle* and *Les Beaux Quartiers.*

Balakian, Anna. *Literary Origins of Surrealism (A New Mysticism in French Poetry),* New York: Kings Crown Press, 1947. Excellent study of literary Surrealism.

——. "The Post-surrealism of Aragon and Eluard," *Yale French Studies,* I, 2 (Fall–Winter, 1948), 93–102. Shows continuity of Surrealism in Aragon's and Eluard's post-Surrealist works.

Becker, Lucille and della Fazia, Alba. "The Versification Techniques of Louis Aragon," *The French Review*, XXXVIII, No. 6 (May, 1965), 734–43. A study of Aragon's technical works on versification and his poetic innovations.

Breton, André. *Manifeste du surréalisme*. Paris: Kra, 1924.

—— *Misère de la poésie ("L'Affaire Aragon" devant l'opinion publique)*. Paris: Editions Surréalistes, 1932. Surrealist defense of Aragon's "Front Rouge."

—— *Entretiens 1913–1952*. Paris: Gallimard, 1952. Valuable insights into Surrealist movement.

Brugmans, H. K. "Aragon, résistant, conteur et poète," *Erasme* I (1946), 210–36. This article links war works to historical events and traces remnants of Surrealism in Aragon's war poetry.

Caute, David. *Communism and the French Intellectuals 1914–60*. London: André Deutsch, 1964. A comprehensive study of the history of the Communist Party in France and its relationship with the intellectuals.

Crastre, Victor. "Le Drame du surréalisme," *Les Temps Modernes*, No. 34 (July, 1948), pp. 42–61 and No. 35 (August, 1948), pp. 290–313. Account of relationship between Surrealists and Communist group of *Clarté*.

Garaudy, Roger. *L'Itinéraire d'Aragon: du surréalisme au monde réel*. Paris: Gallimard, 1961. This study includes unpublished documents from the library of Jacques Doucet.

Gavillet, André. *La Littérature au défi: Aragon surréaliste*. (Essai sur la fonction de la parole). Fribourg: La Baconnière, 1957. In addition to its study of Aragon's Surrealist works, this volume contains a comprehensive bibliography up to 1957, on pp. 313–30.

Gindine, Yvette. *Aragon, prosateur surréaliste*. Geneva: Droz, 1966. Detailed study of Aragon's Surrealist prose works: *Anicet ou le Panorama roman*, *Les Aventures de Télémaque*, *Le Libertinage*, *Le Paysan de Paris*, and *Le Traité du style*.

Good, Thomas. "Out of the Darkness: Louis Aragon in the Years of the Occupation," *Transformation*, III, 1945, 158–64. Study of *Le Crève-coeur* and *Les Yeux d'Elsa*.

Haroche, Charles. *L'Idée de l'amour dans "Le Fou d'Elsa" et l'oeuvre d'Aragon*. Paris: Gallimard, 1966. Literary essay devoted to a study of *Le Fou d'Elsa* which the critic considers to be the key to all of Aragon's work.

Josephson, Hannah and Cowley, Malcolm. Editors. *Aragon: Poet of the French Resistance*. New York: Duell, Sloan and Pearce, 1945. Collection of articles on Aragon and translations of his war poetry, essays, and stories.

Juin, Hubert. *Aragon*. Paris: Gallimard, 1960. Concise introduction to Aragon's work. It contains a fine reference section comprising a biography of the author, an anthology, selected quotations from and résumés of his work, an interview with the critic and a bibliography.

Lescure, Pierre de. *Aragon romancier*. Paris: Gallimard, 1960. Discussion of novels of "The Real World" and *La Semaine Sainte*.

Nadeau, Maurice. *Histoire du surréalisme*. Paris: Editions du Seuil, 1946. Trans. as *The History of Surrealism* by Richard Howard. New York: The Macmillan Company, 1965. Comprehensive history of Dada and Surrealism, followed by selected texts.

Peyre, Henri. "The Resistance and Literary Revival in France," *Yale Review*, XXXV, No. 1 (Sept., 1945), 85–92.

Picon, Gaëtan. *Panorama de la nouvelle littérature française*. Paris: Gallimard, 1949. Excellent short studies of Aragon's work until 1949.

Raillard, Georges. *Aragon*. Paris: Editions Universitaires, 1964. This work is part of a collection, "Classiques du XXème siècle." Good introduction to Aragon's work through *Le Fou d'Elsa*.

Raymond, Marcel. *De Baudelaire au surréalisme*. Paris: Corti, 1947.

Roudiez, Léon. "The Case of Louis Aragon and Surrealism," *French Review*, XXVI, No. 2 (December, 1952), 96–104. The thesis of this article is that Aragon was never truly a Surrealist, that his Surrealist texts continually revealed more continuity and art than other Surrealist works.

Roy, Claude. *Aragon*. Paris: Seghers (Poètes d'aujourd'hui), 1962. This work adheres to the format of the entire collection which is devoted to pre-eminent poets. It opens with an introduction to the life and work of the poet, followed by a chronological presentation of selected poems.

———. "Aragon, romancier," *Europe*. March, 1948. Reprinted in *Descriptions Critiques*. Paris: Gallimard, 1949. Discussion of *Les Beaux Quartiers* and *Les Voyageurs de l'impériale*.

Simon, Pierre-Henri. *L'Esprit et l'histoire*. Paris: Armand Colin, 1954. Discussion of *Les Communistes*.

Sur, Jean. *Aragon: le réalisme de l'amour*. Paris: Centurion, 1966. This work belongs to a series of critical works which, under the general heading "Humanisme et Religion," deal with writers who are preoccupied with religious or spiritual problems. This work is limited to a discussion of the philosophical implications of Aragon's work.

Index

Index

Louis XVIII, 72, 74, 76
Love: courtly, 82; jealousy, 106, 107; justification of life, 113; language of the novel, 102, 103; man's greatest invention, 108, 109, 111; religion of, 17, 30, 59, 78, 79, 80, 81, 91, 96; salvation by, 31, 32, 36; surrealist, 16, 17. *See also* Couple
Lumière de Stendhal, La, 57

Madame Bovary, 36
Mailer, Norman, 107
Manon Lescaut, 36
Marx, Karl, 61
Mauriac, 36
Maurois, 23, 36
Mayakovsky, 17, 18, 24
Mentor (*Les Aventures de Télémaque*), 32
Mercadier, Pascal (*Les Voyageurs de l'impériale*), 64
Mercadier, Pierre (*Les Voyageurs de l'impériale*), 62, 63, 64
Mirabelle (*Anicet ou le Panorama roman*), 30, 31
Mise à mort, La, 75, 77, 102–8, 113
"Misère de la poésie," 20
Moncy, Jean de (*Les Communistes*), 69, 70, 76, 83
"Monde réel, Le," 53, 57, 58, 62, 64, 65, 69, 77, 83, 103, 113
"Morale courtoise," 46
Morocco, 19, 54
Mouvement perpétuel, Le, 26, 27, 28
Musée Grévin, Le, 46

Napoleon, 72, 74, 76
Napoleon, Louis, 46
Naturalism, 57
Nettencourt, Diane de (*Les Cloches de Bâle*), 53, 54, 60
Nizan, Paul, 22
Nouveau Crève-Coeur, Le, 50, 51, 64
Novel, theory of, 102–11

Old Age, theme of, 64, 86, 87, 93, 95, 102
Orfilat, Patrice (*Les Communistes*), 22
Orpheus, 104

Paris, 26, 33, 34, 44, 58, 59, 66, 72, 74, 94, 95
"Passage de l'Opéra, Le," 30, 34
Pasternak, Boris, 102
Paysan de Paris, Le, 17, 30, 33, 34–36, 61, 107, 113
Peinture au défi, La, 37, 76, 96
Péri, Gabriel, 49, 81
Persécuté persécuteur, 38, 39, 40, 113
Pétain, 19
Petitjeanin, Abbé (*Les Beaux Quartiers*), 59
Petrarch, 45, 81
Picasso, 30, 31, 74
Poètes, Les, 92–94
Pour un réalisme socialiste, 15, 18

Quesnel, Joseph (*Les Beaux Quartiers*), 60, 66, 67, 103

Racine, 66
Resistance, 47, 48, 80
Reverdy, 30
Révolution d'abord et toujours, La, 19
Révolution surréaliste, La, 18, 83
"Rime en 1940, La," 41, 43, 45
Rimbaud, 29, 30, 36, 71
Roman inachevé, Le, 14, 16, 20, 88–89, 92
Rouge et le Noir, Le, 57
Russian revolution, 18

Semaine sainte, La, 5, 14, 72–77, 113
"Sentiment de la nature aux Buttes-Chaumont, Le," 34
Servitude et Grandeur des Français, 23, 48
Shakespeare, 42
Simonidzé, Catherine (*Les Cloches de Bâle*), 14, 53, 54, 55, 56, 67, 73
Sinyavsky, 24
Socialist Realism, 5, 14, 24, 76, 107, 112; theoretical works on, 56–57
"Songe du Paysan, Le," 36
Soupault, Philippe, 14, 15
Stalin, 107
Stendhal, 13, 57, 72
Stevenson, Robert Louis, 103